100 PAGE COLOURING BOOK FLOWER

CRYSTAL
COLORING BOOKS

ISBN: 9798692605900

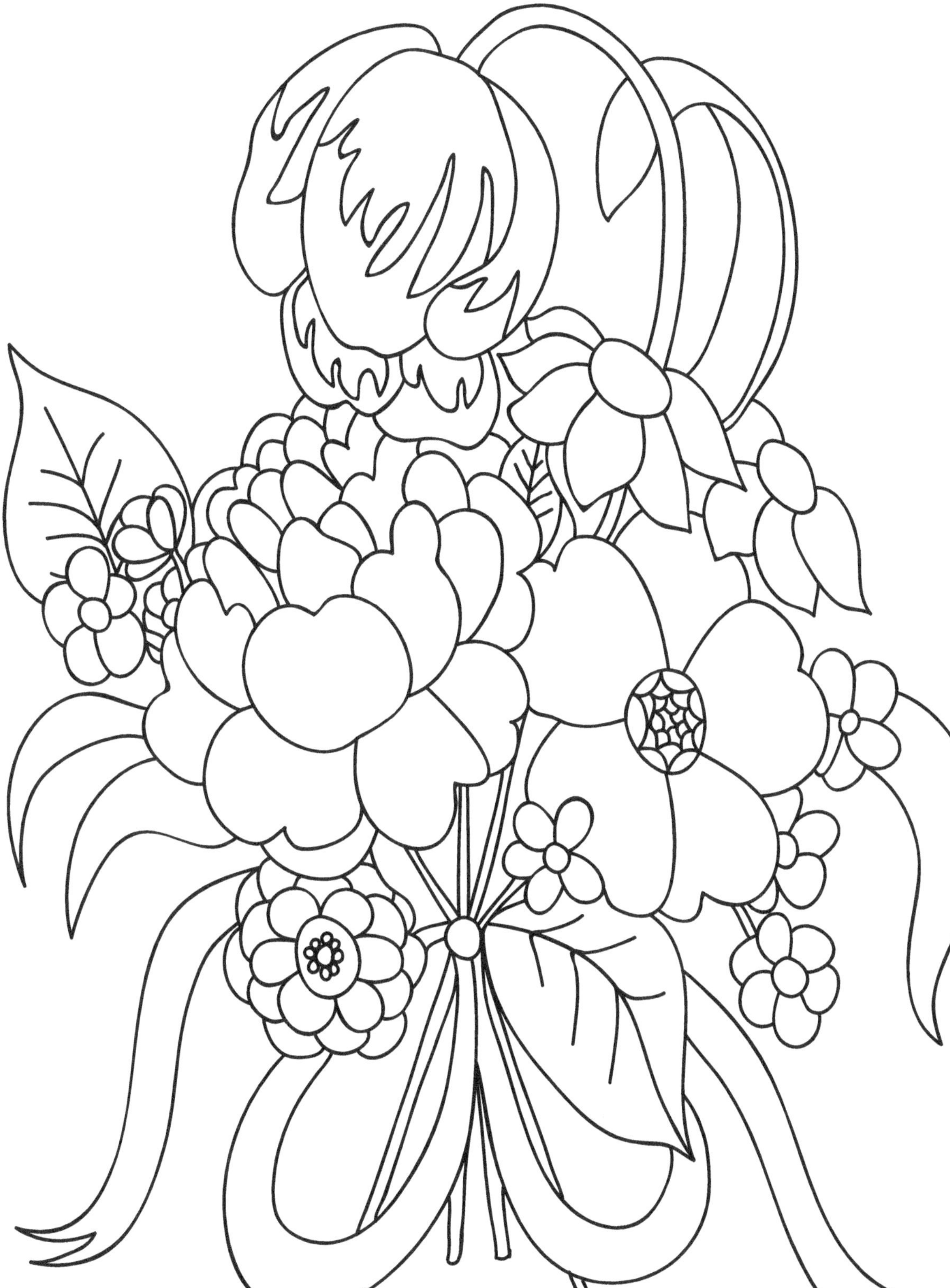

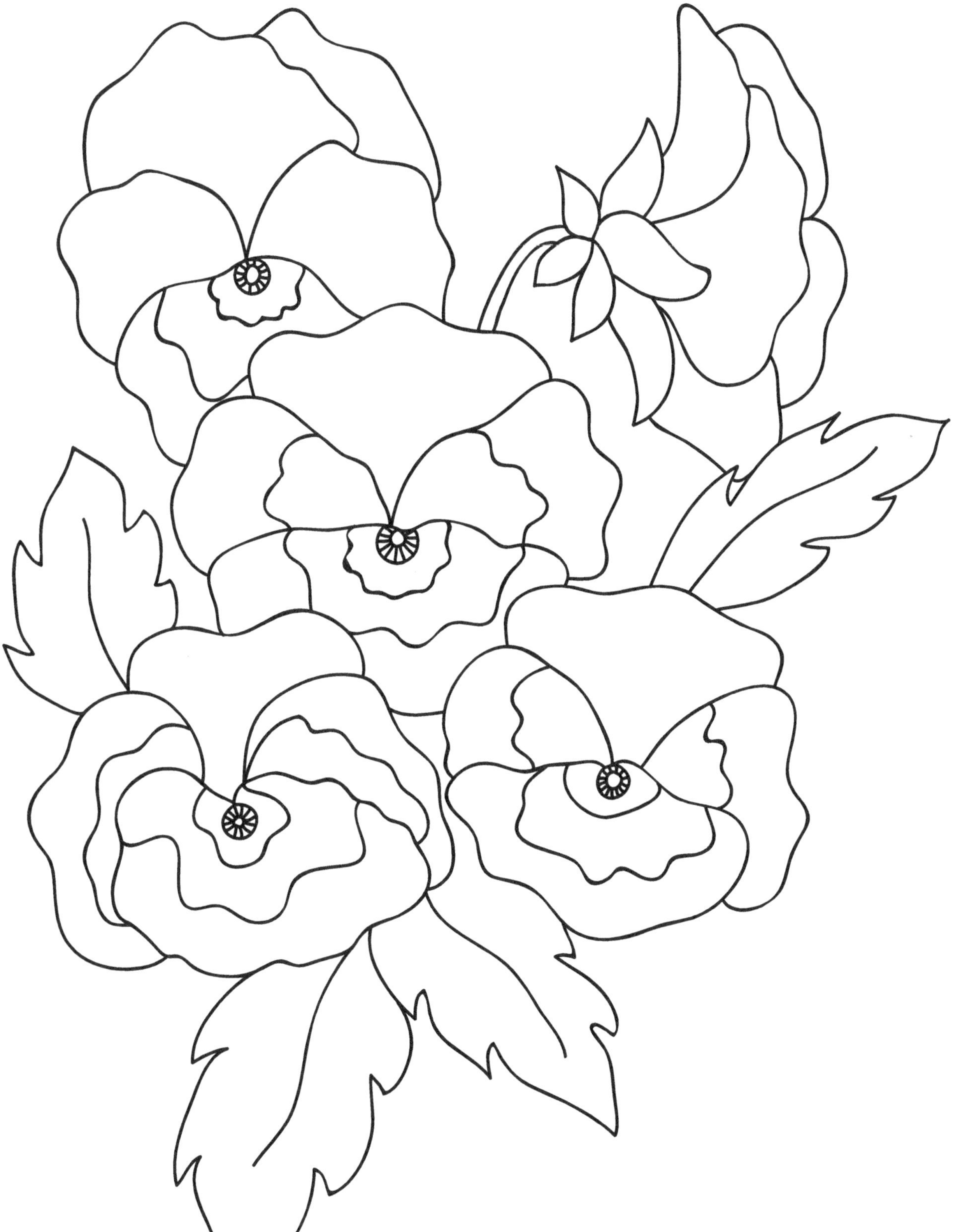

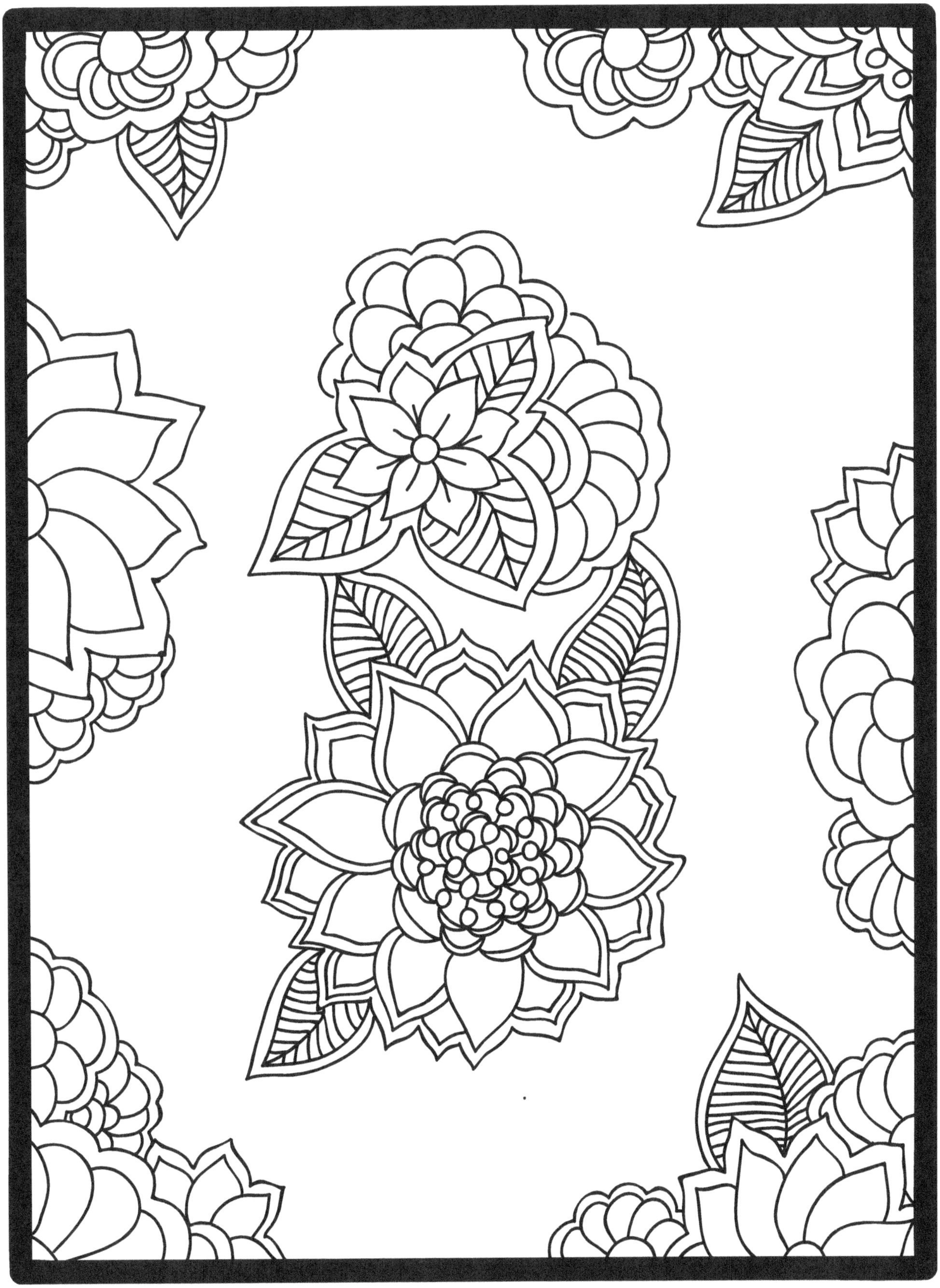

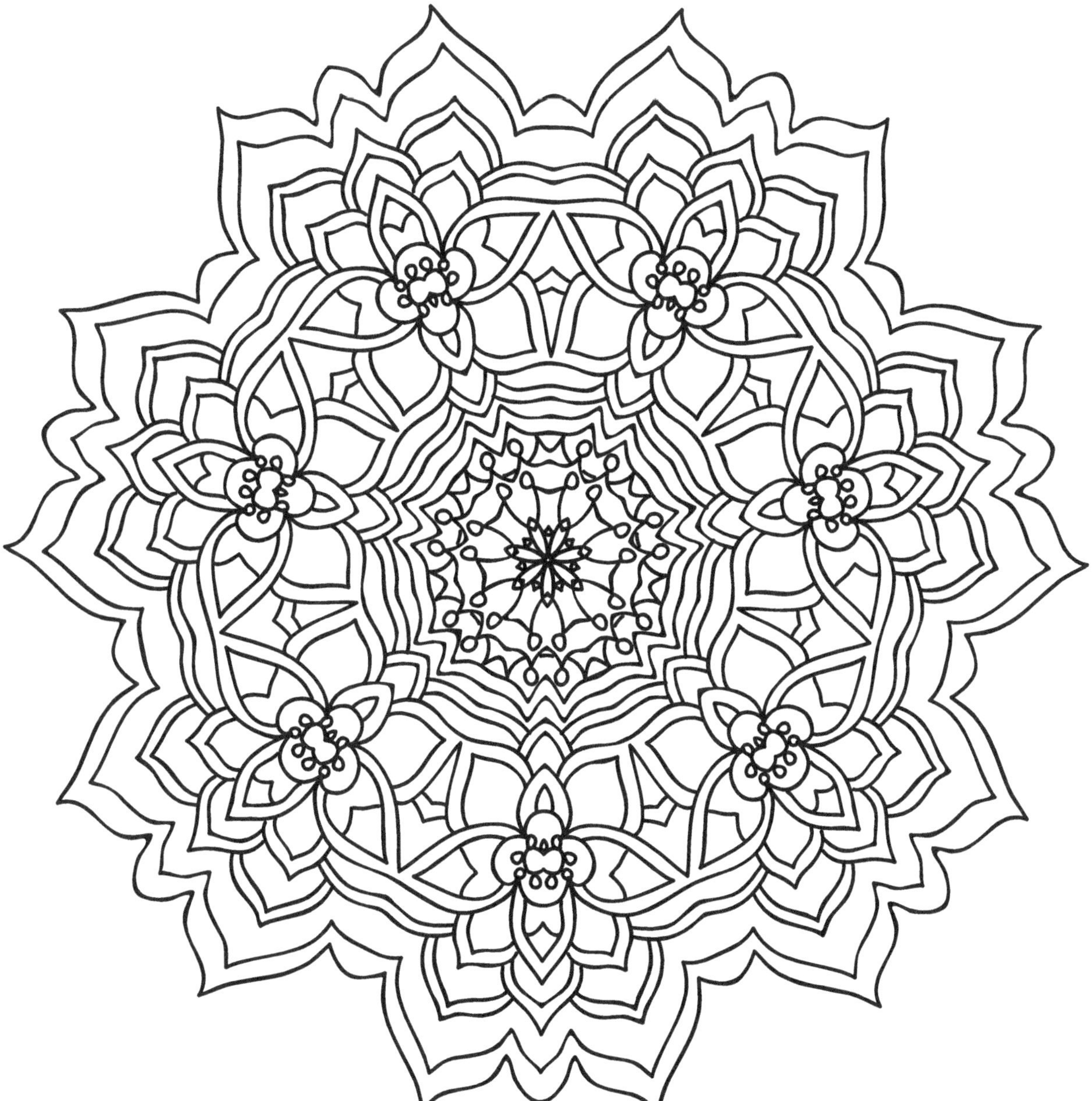

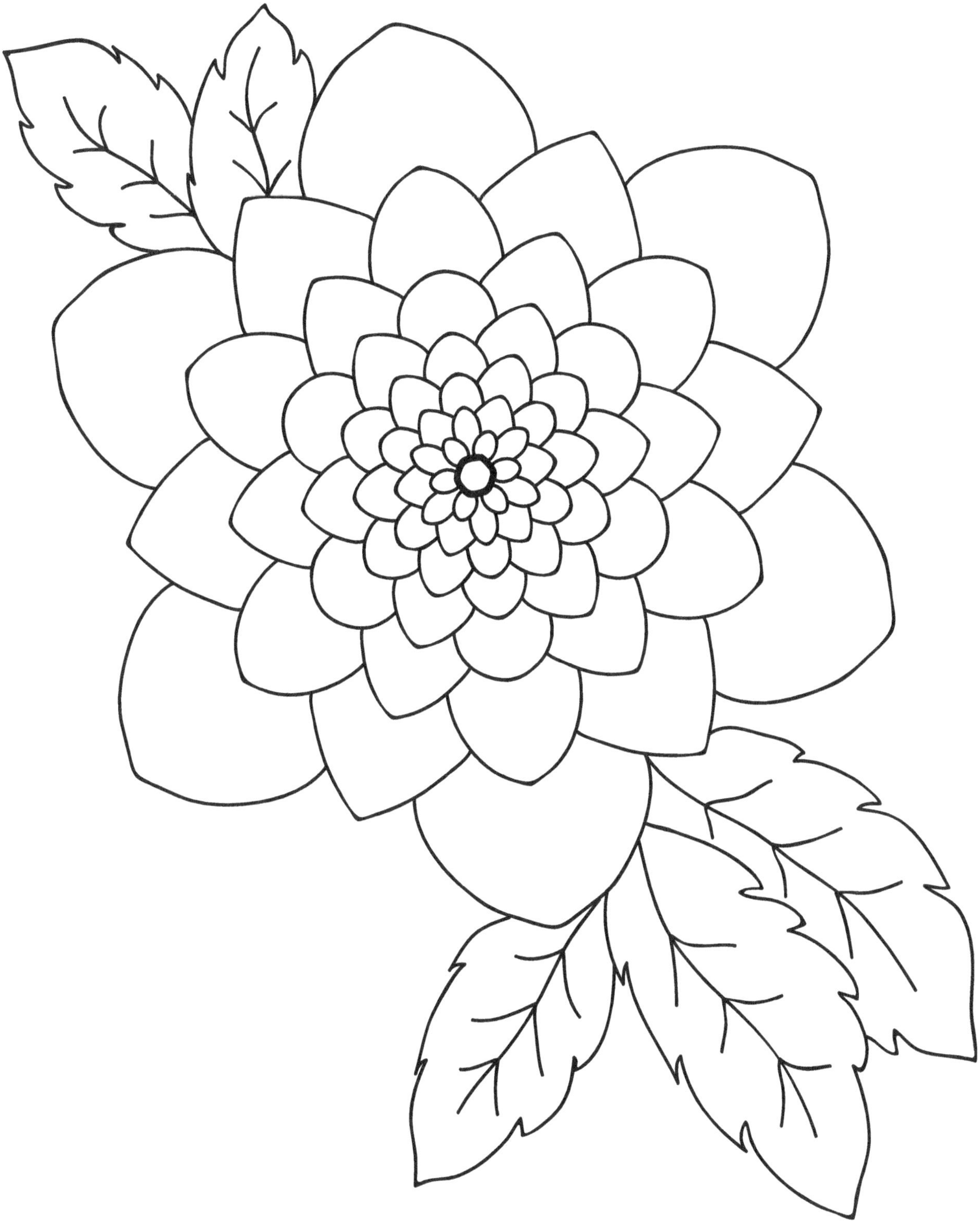

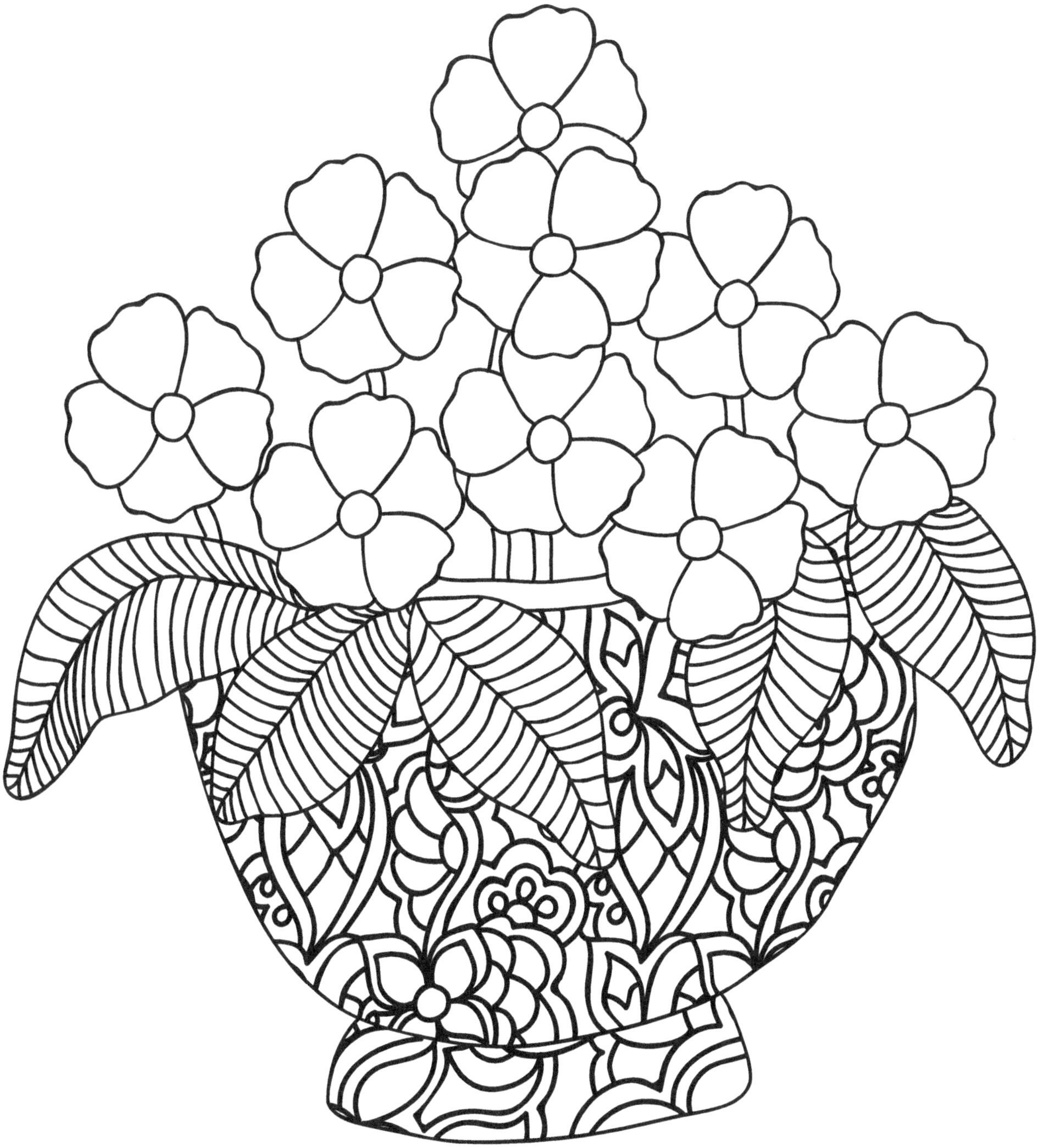

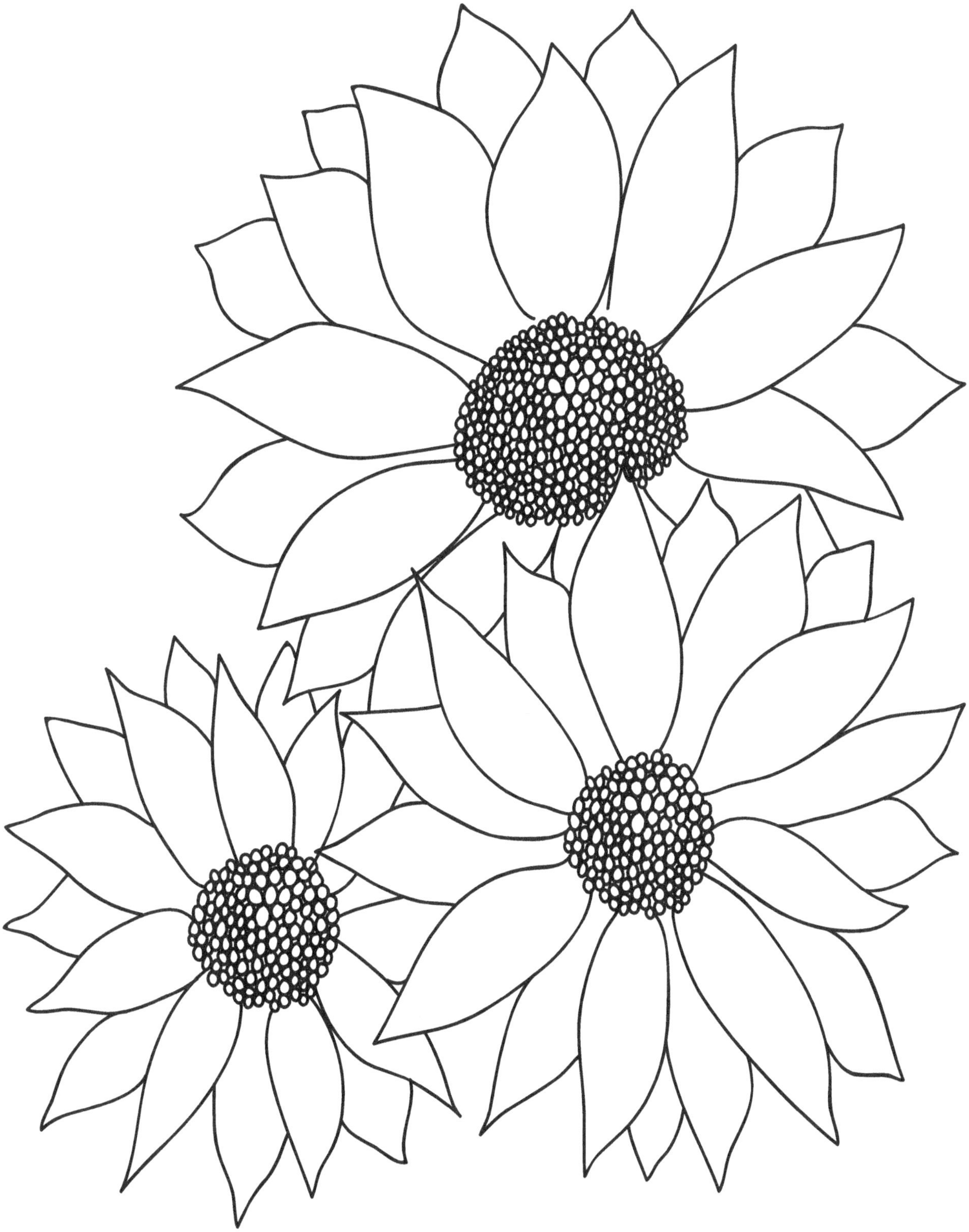

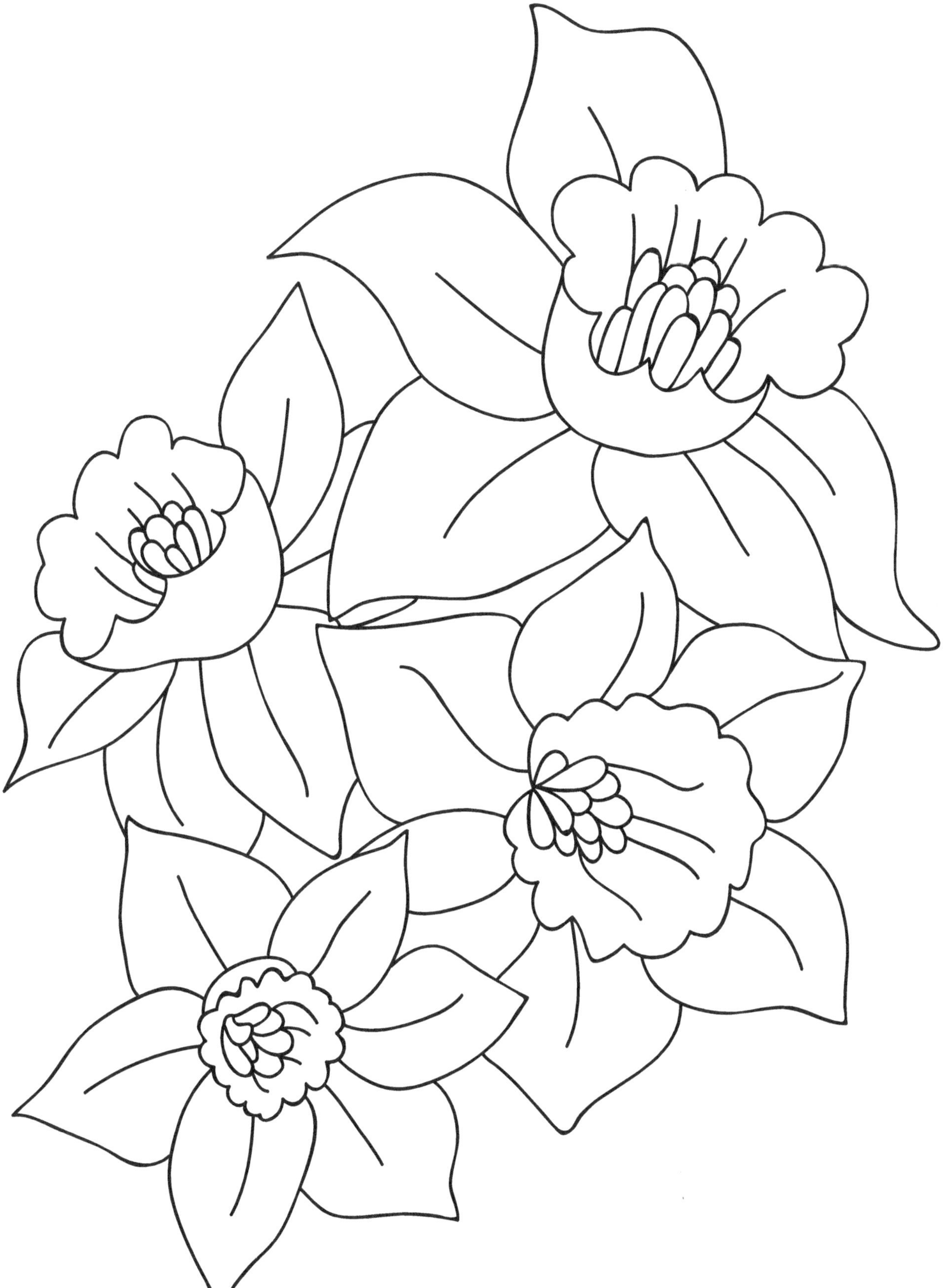

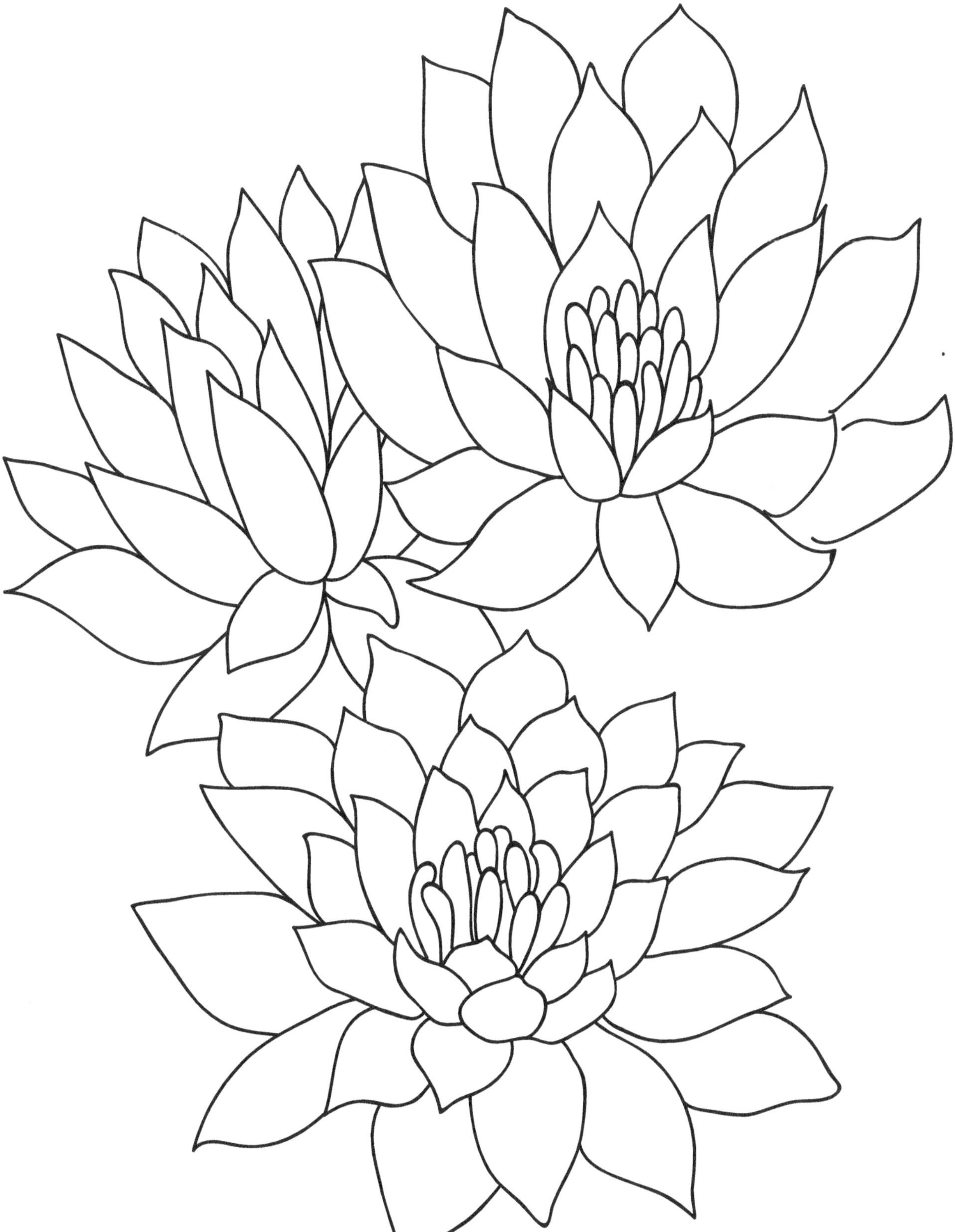

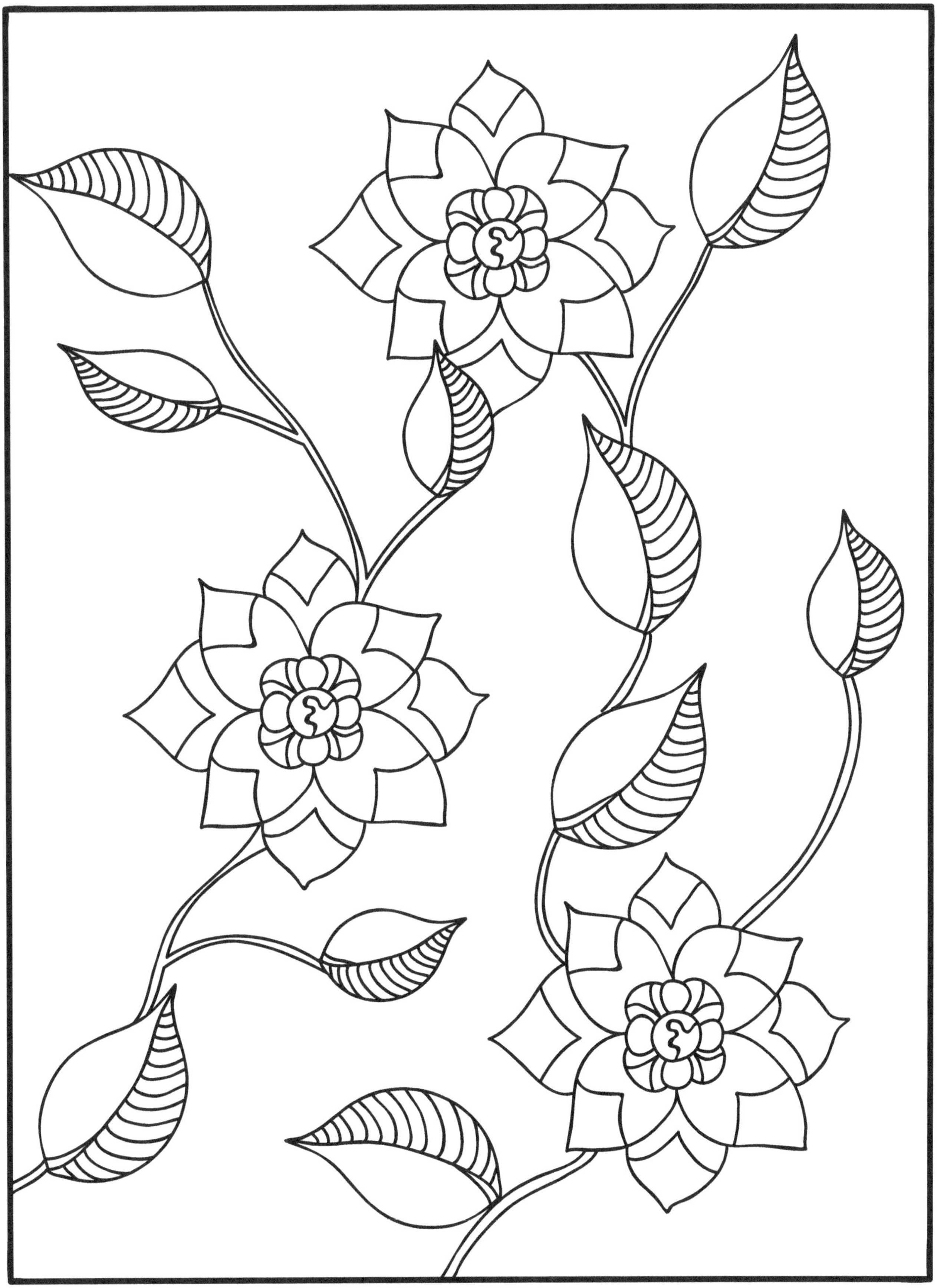

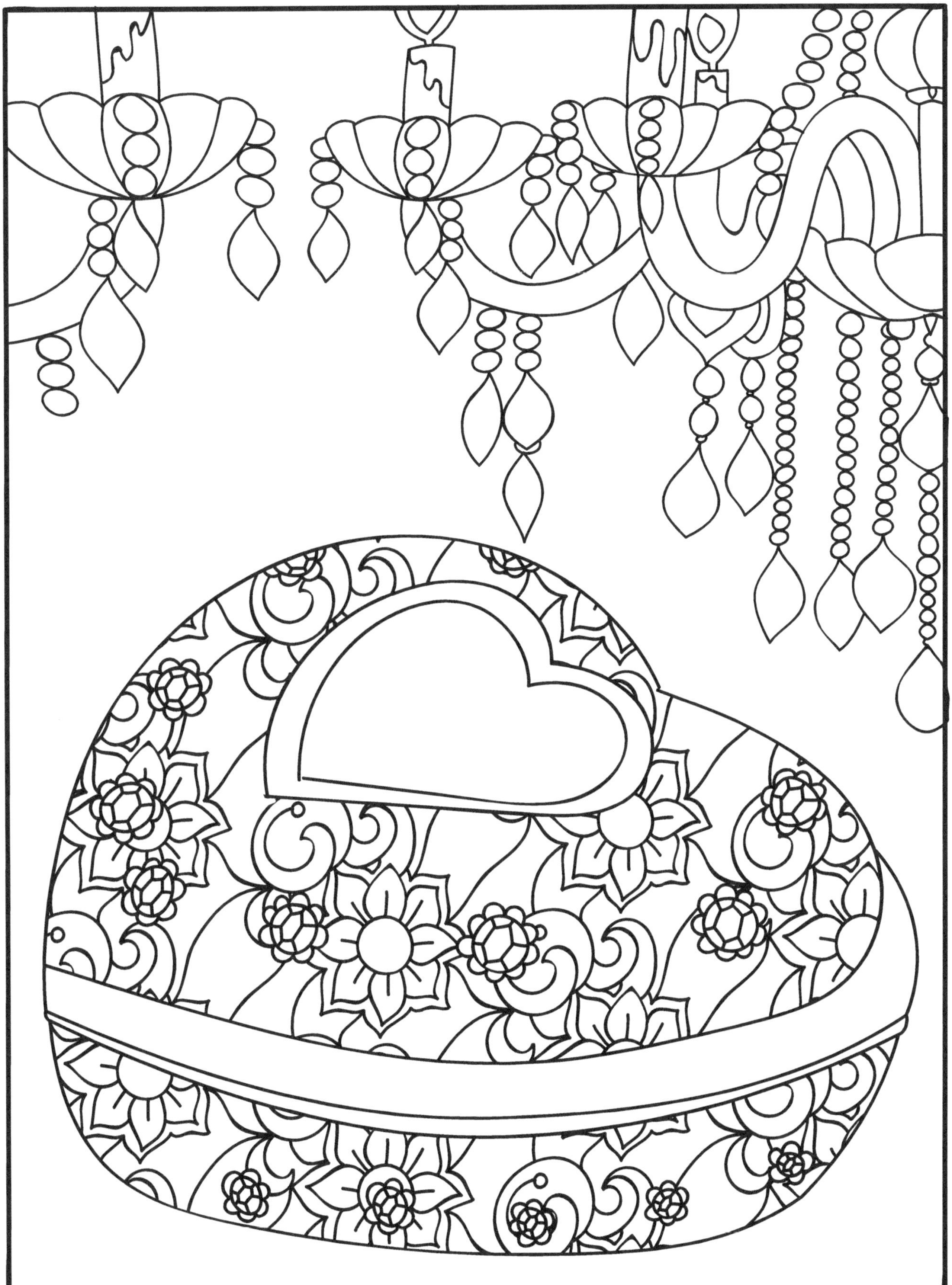

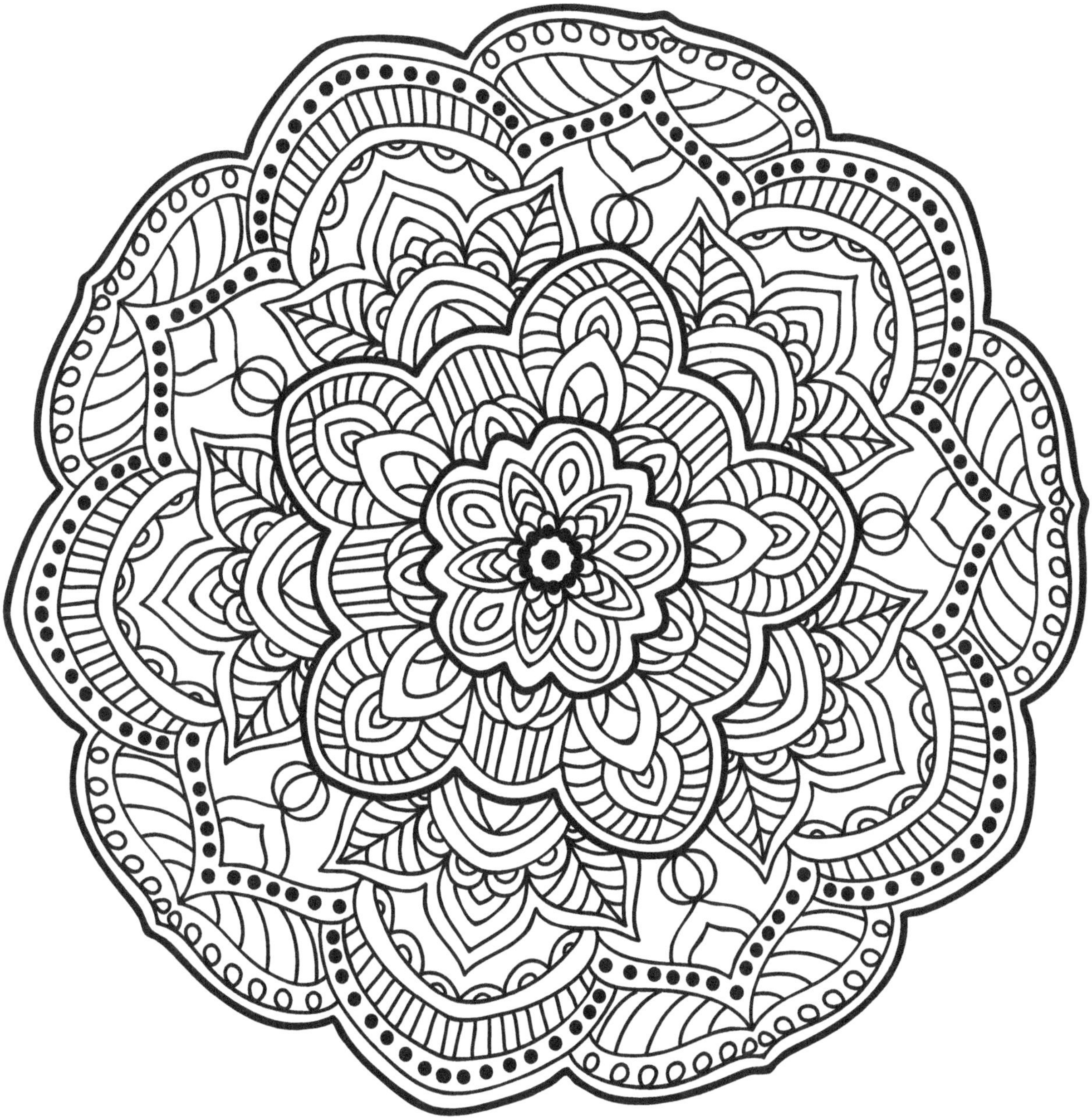

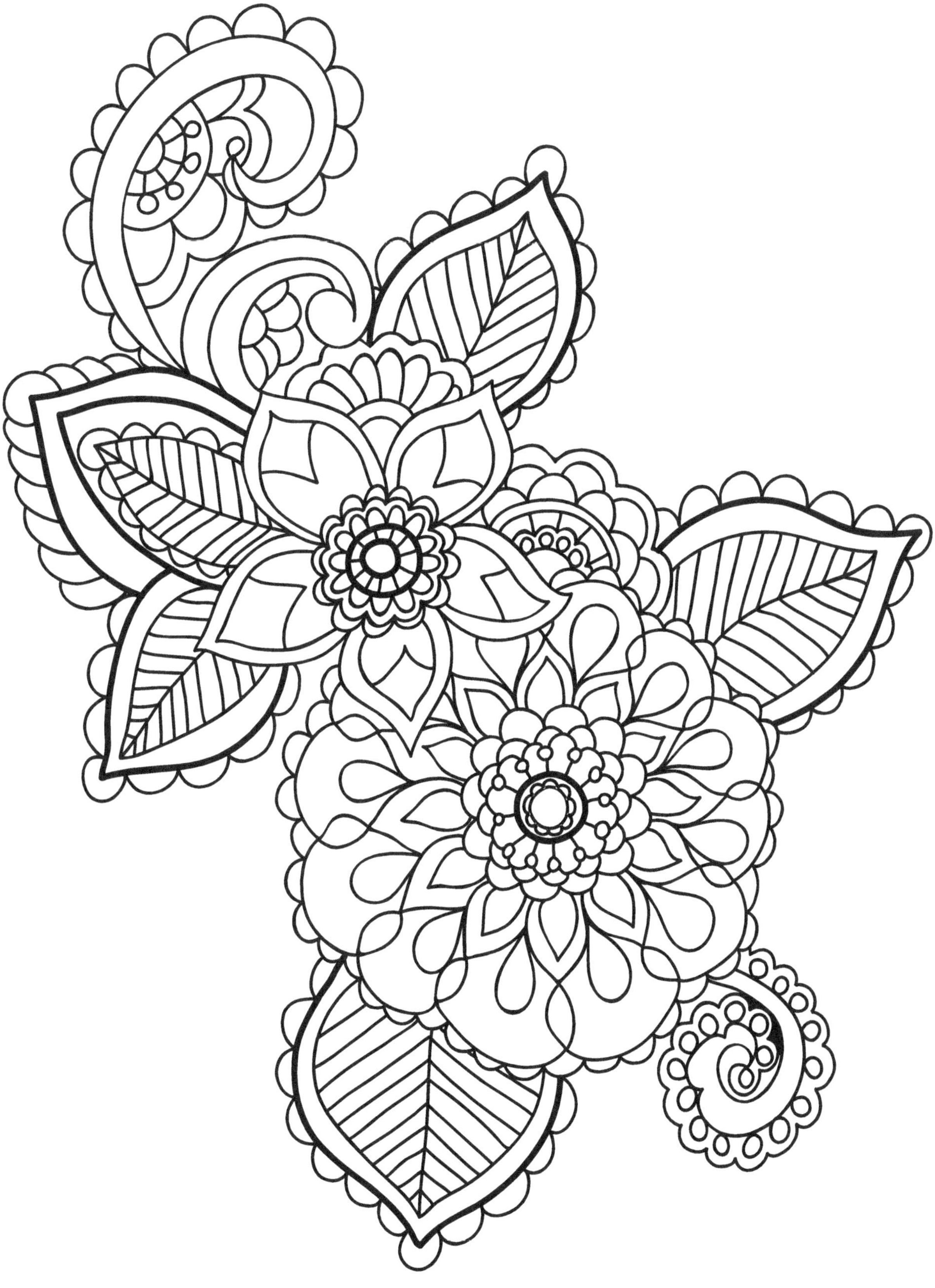

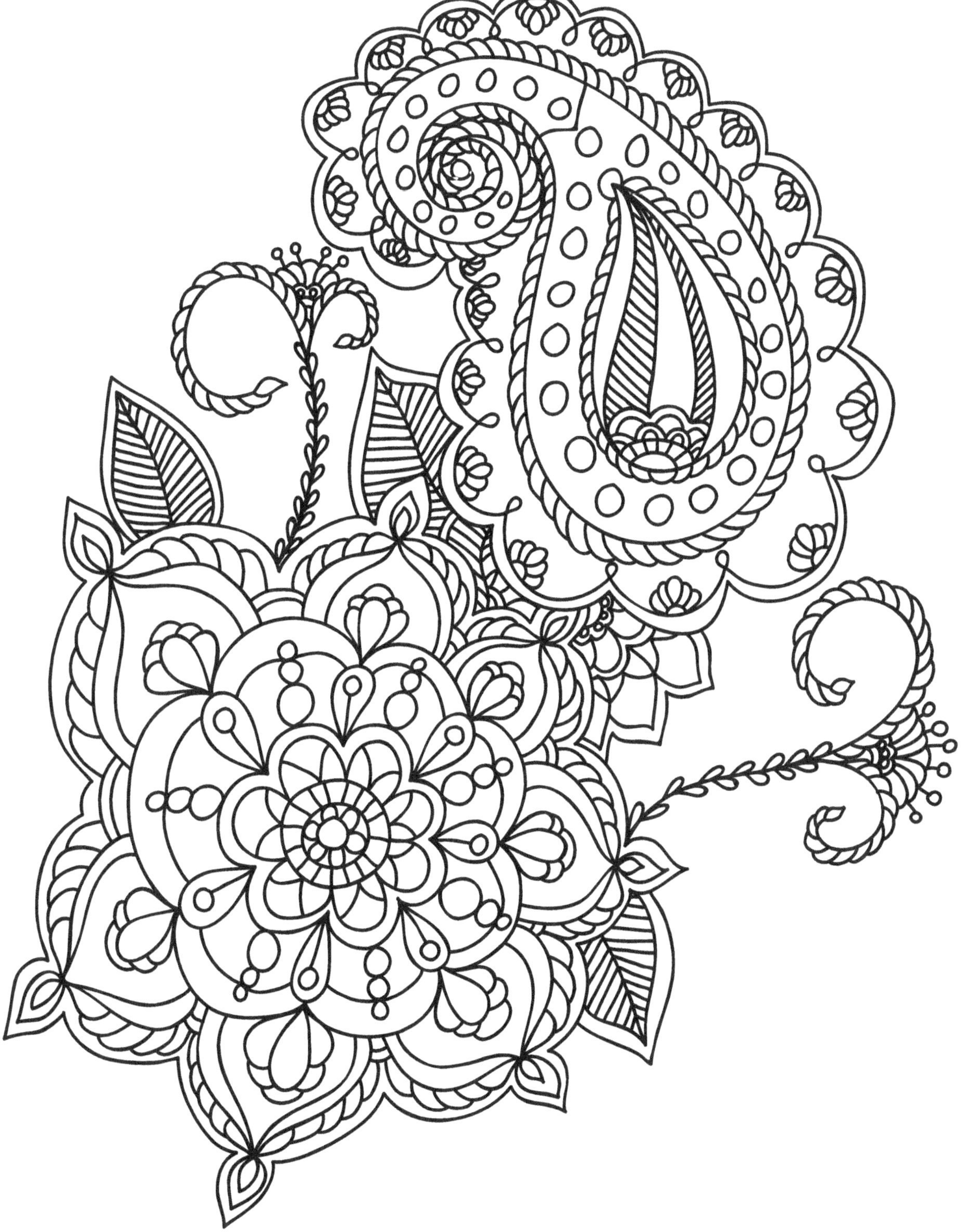

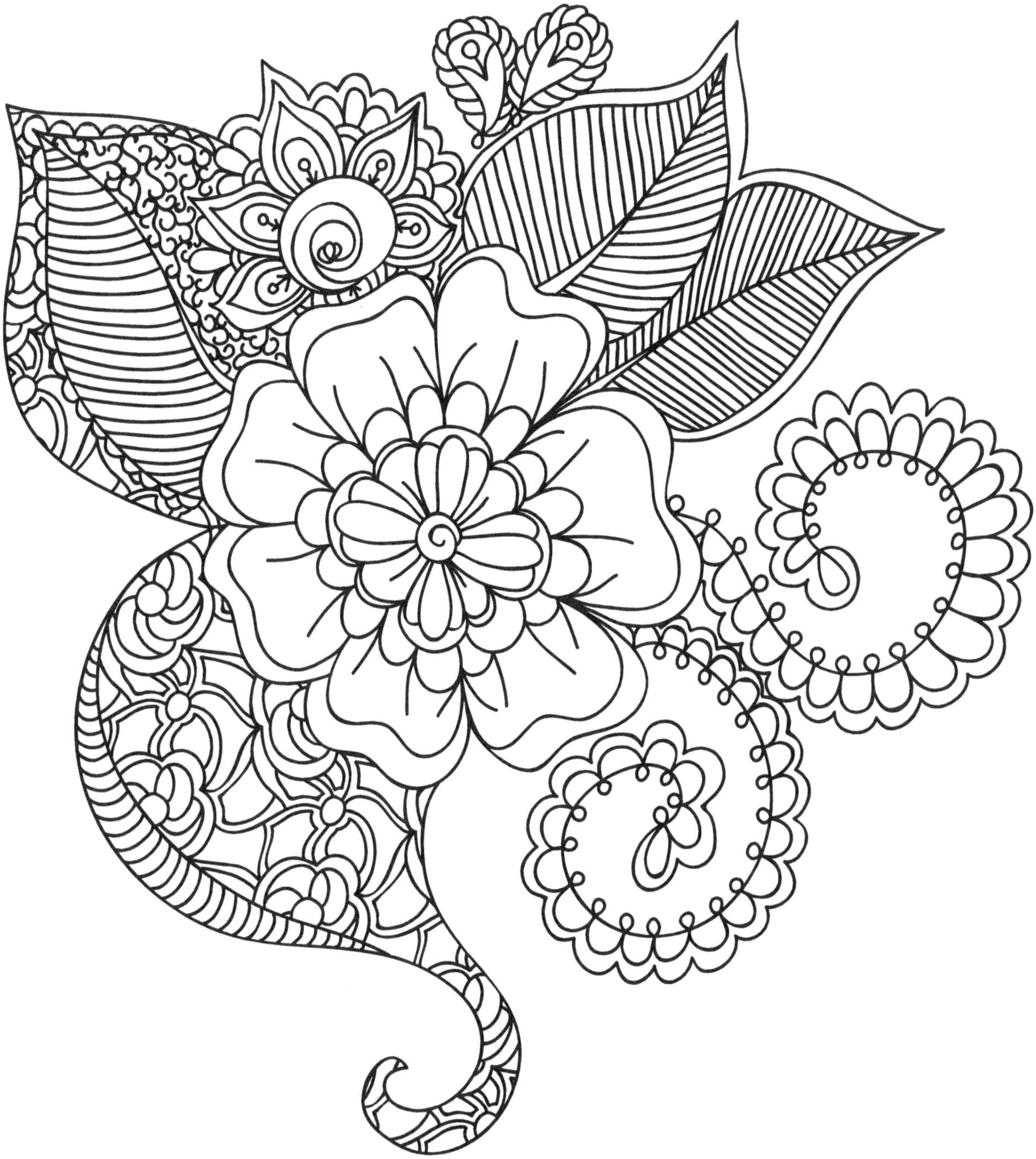

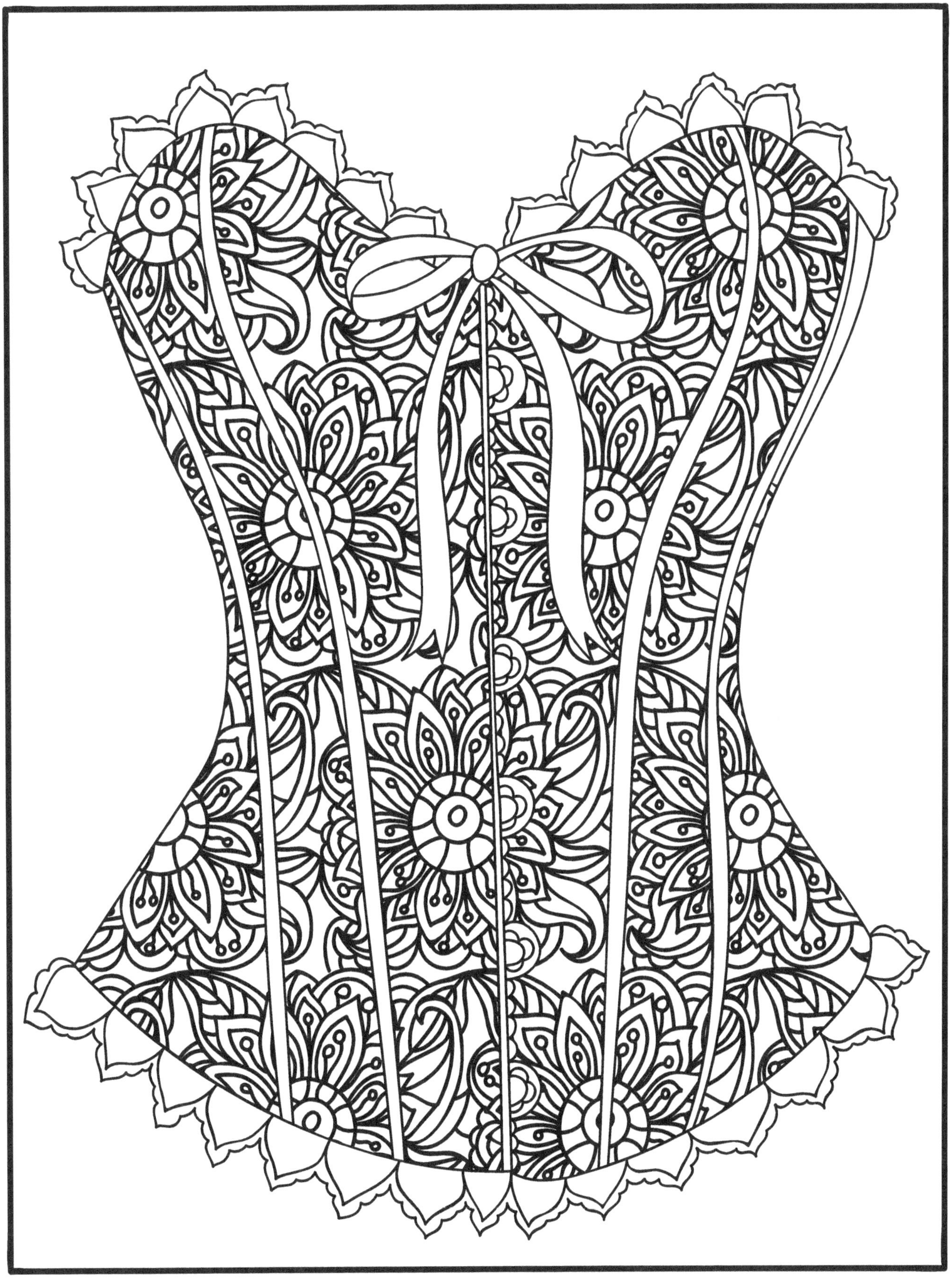

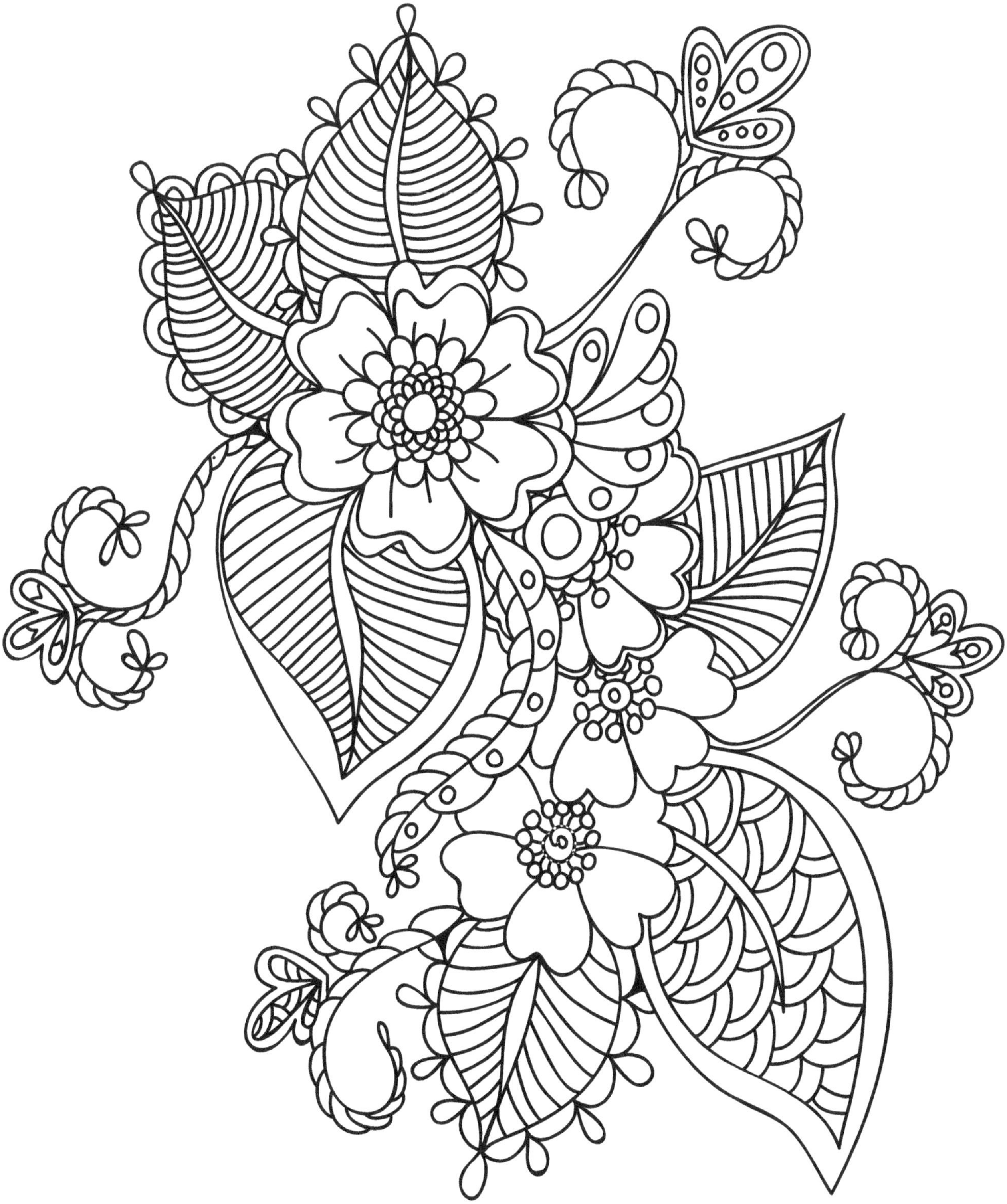

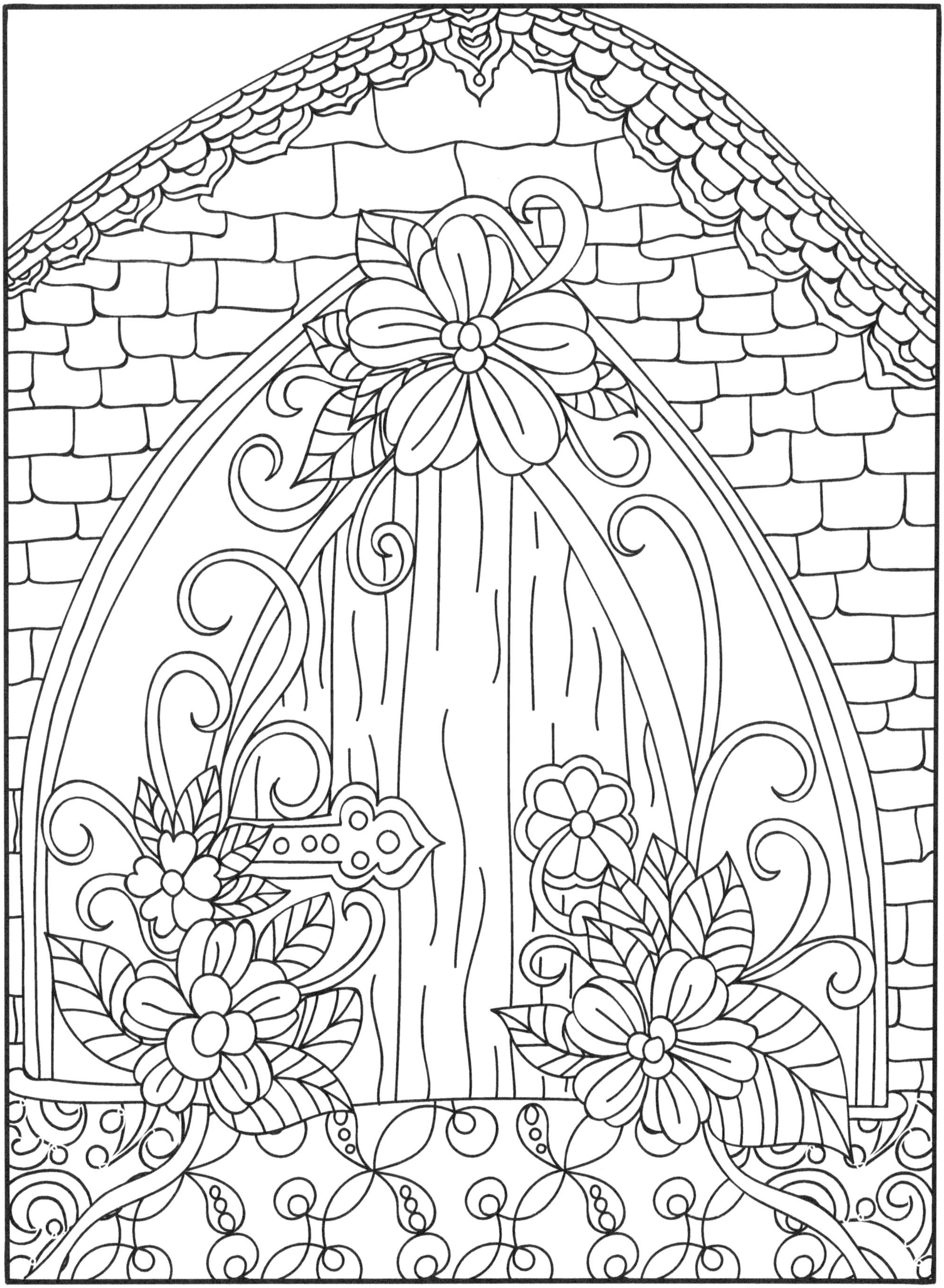

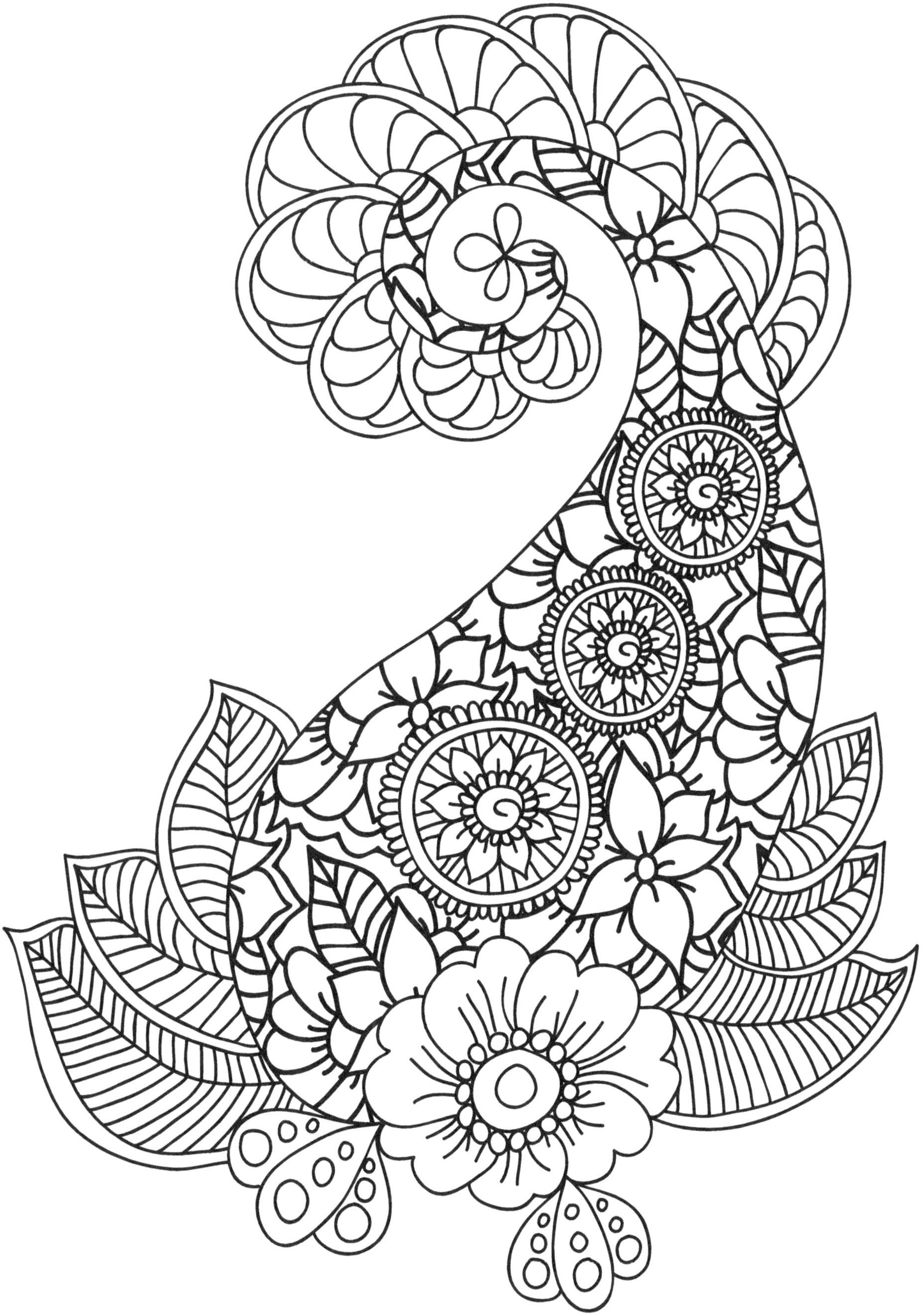

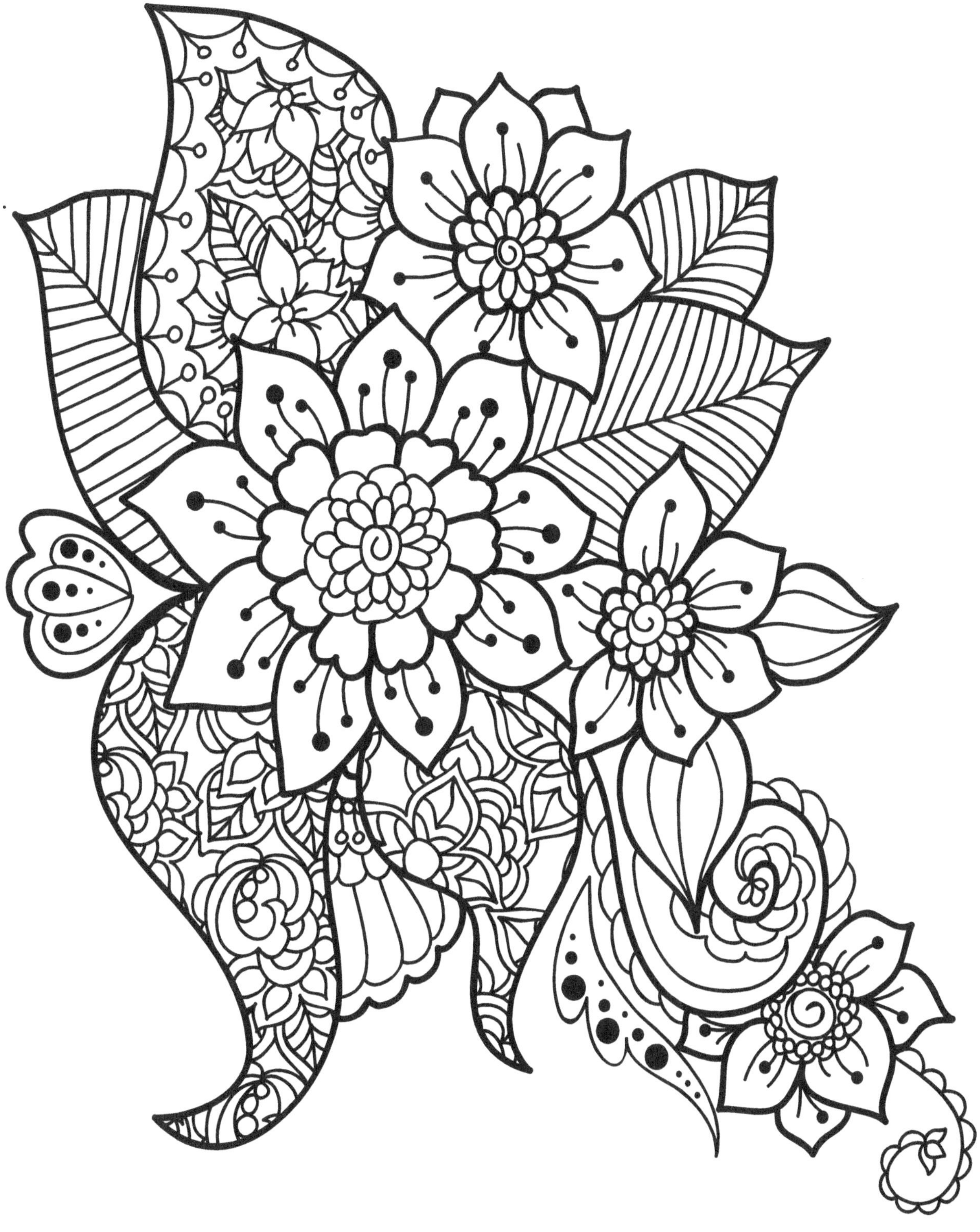

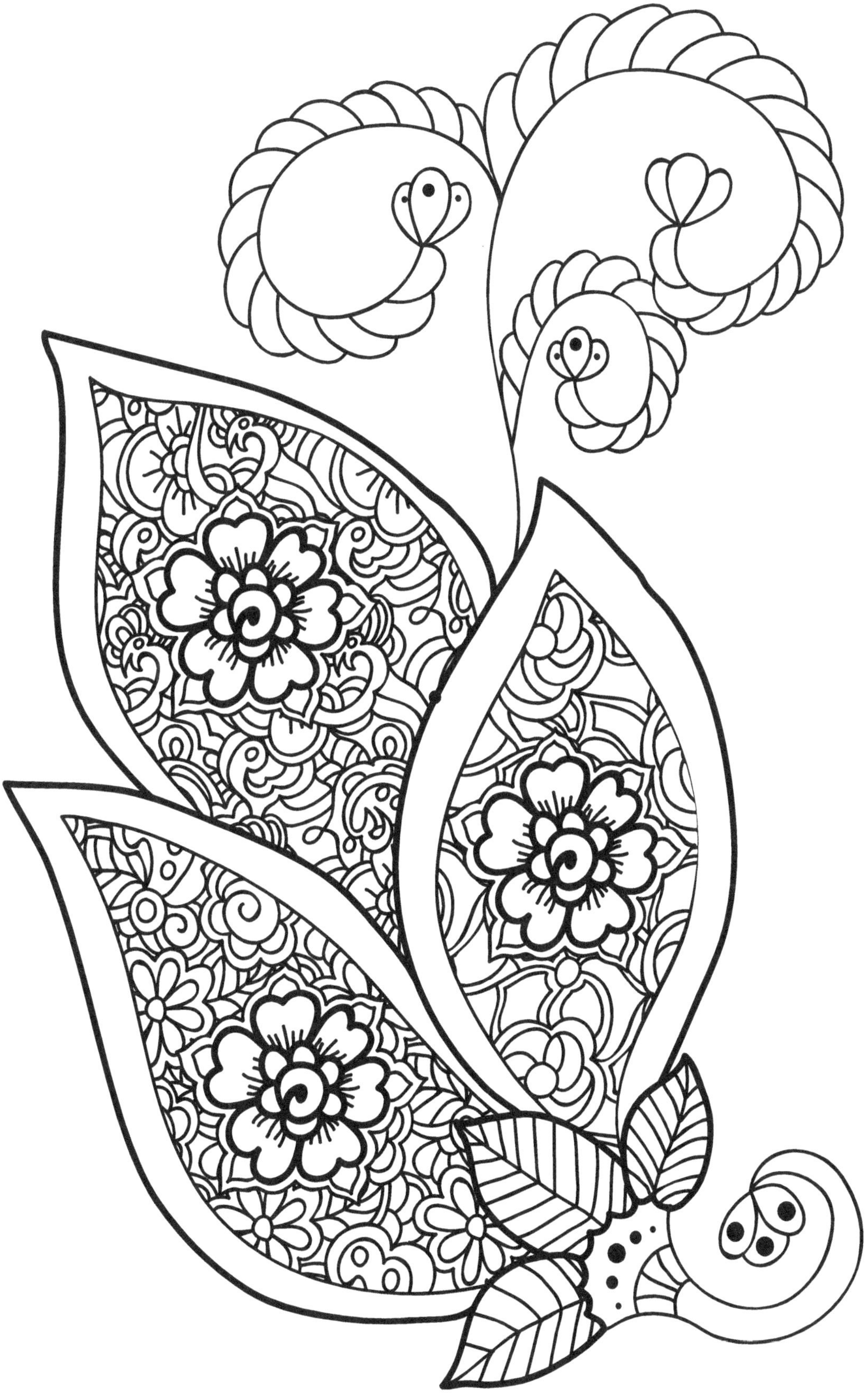

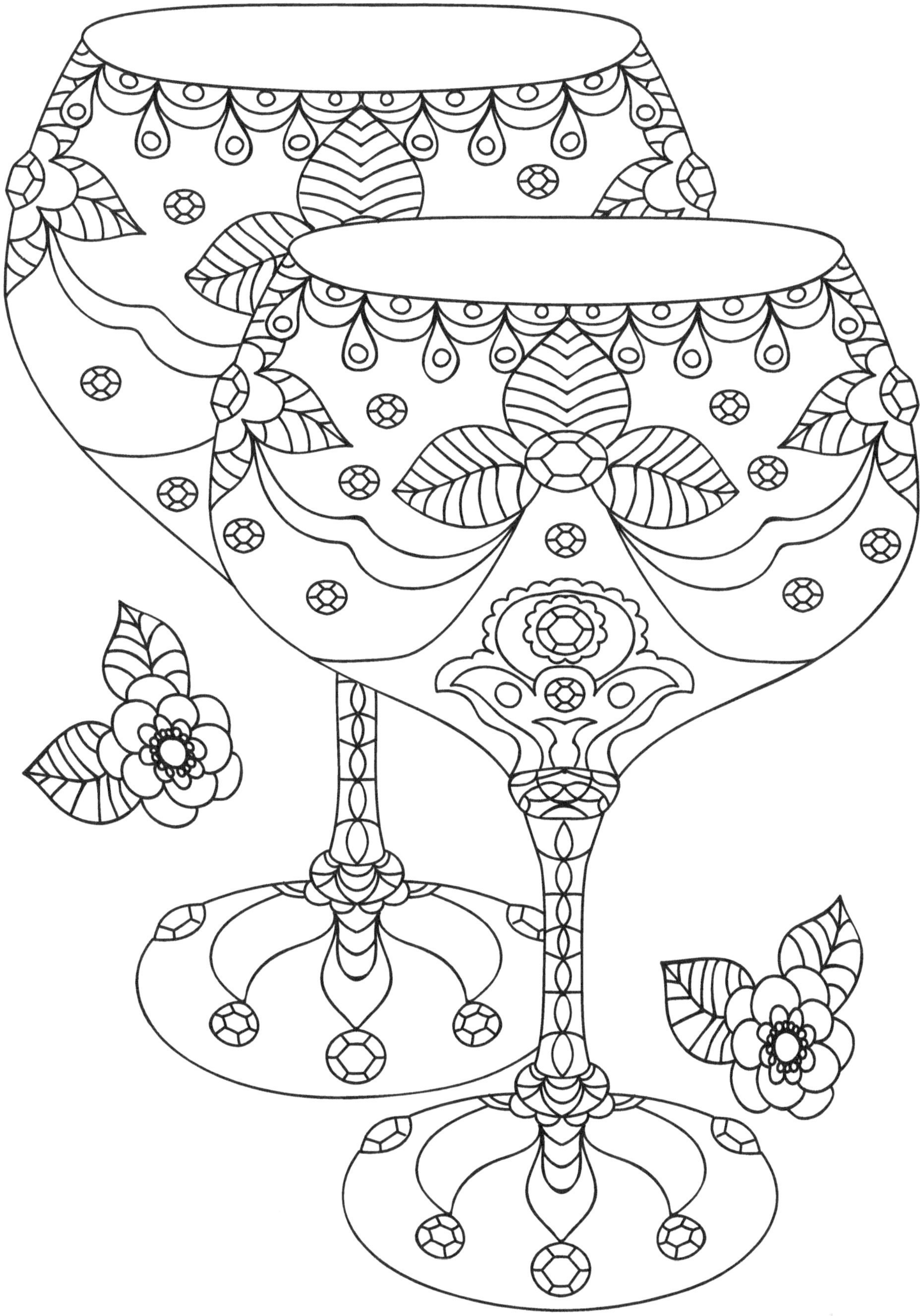

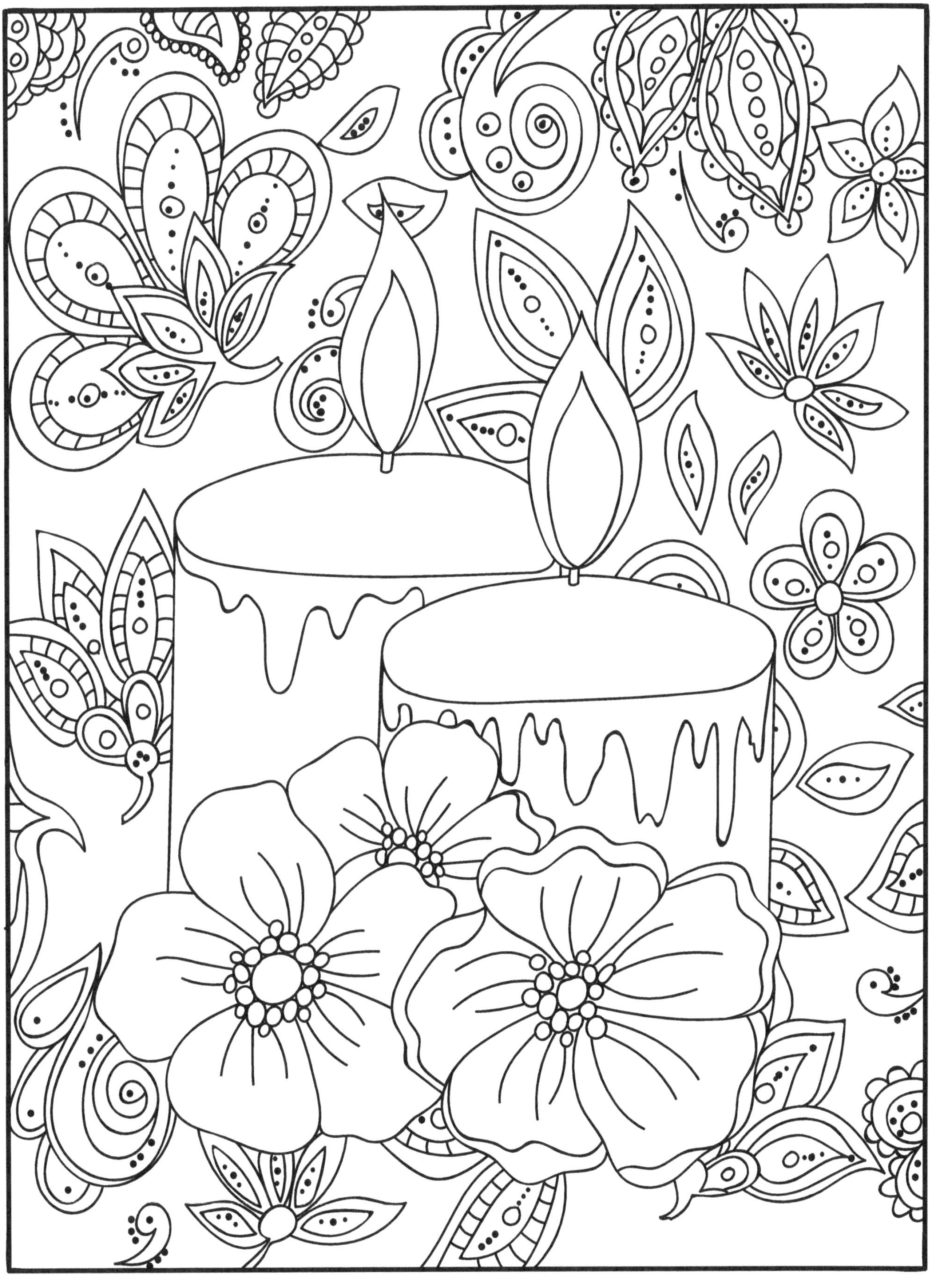

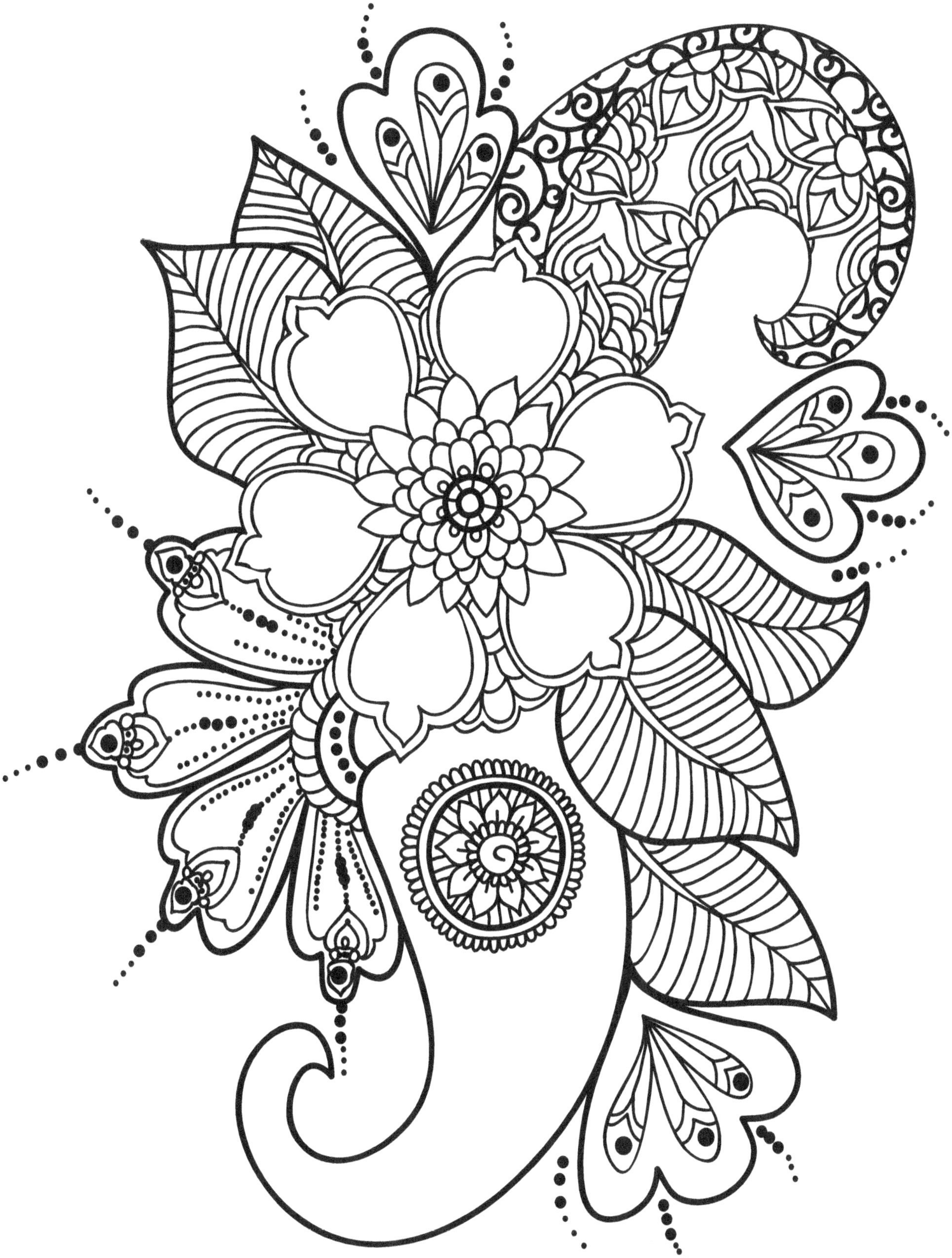

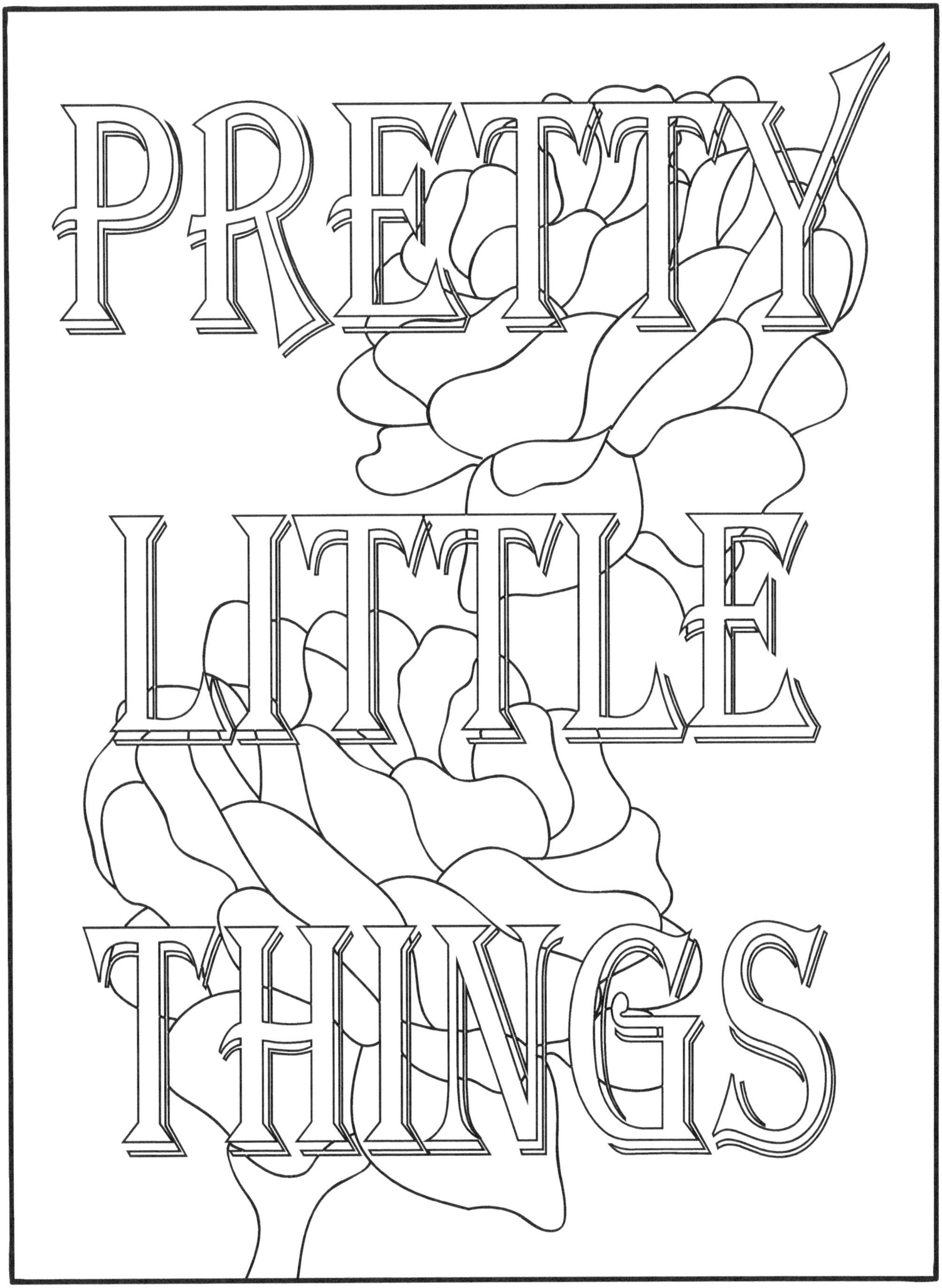
PRETTY
LITTLE
THINGS

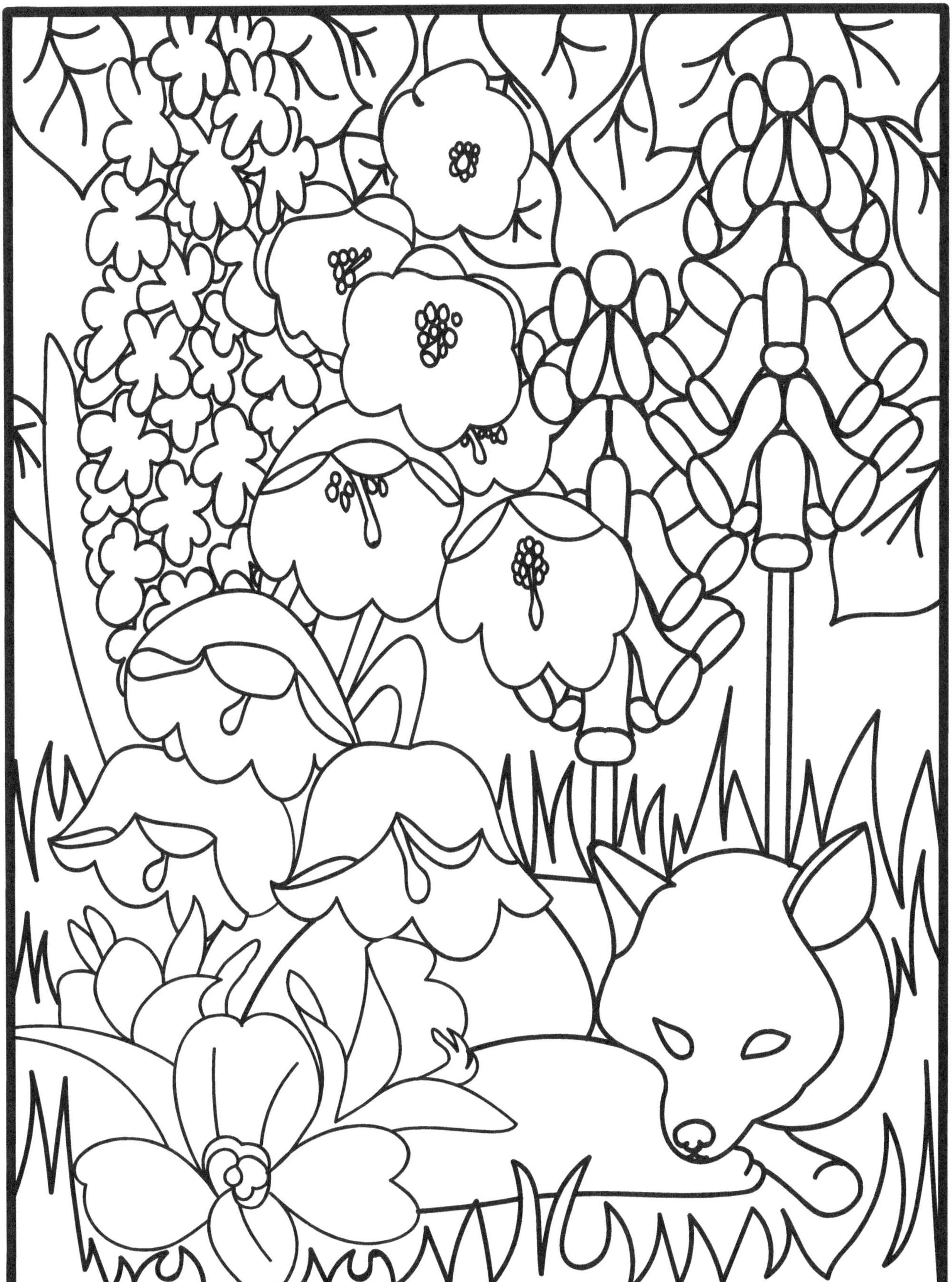

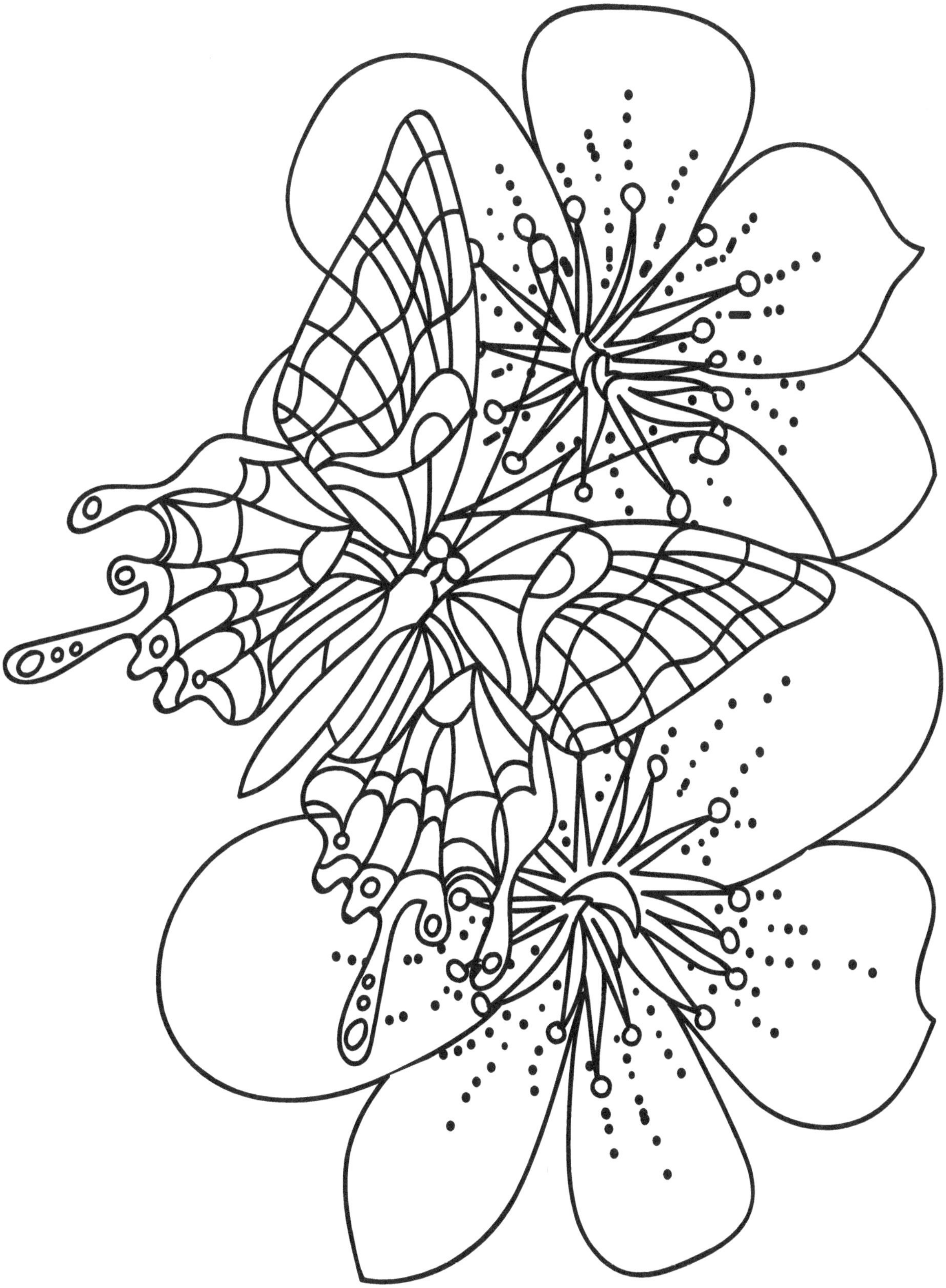

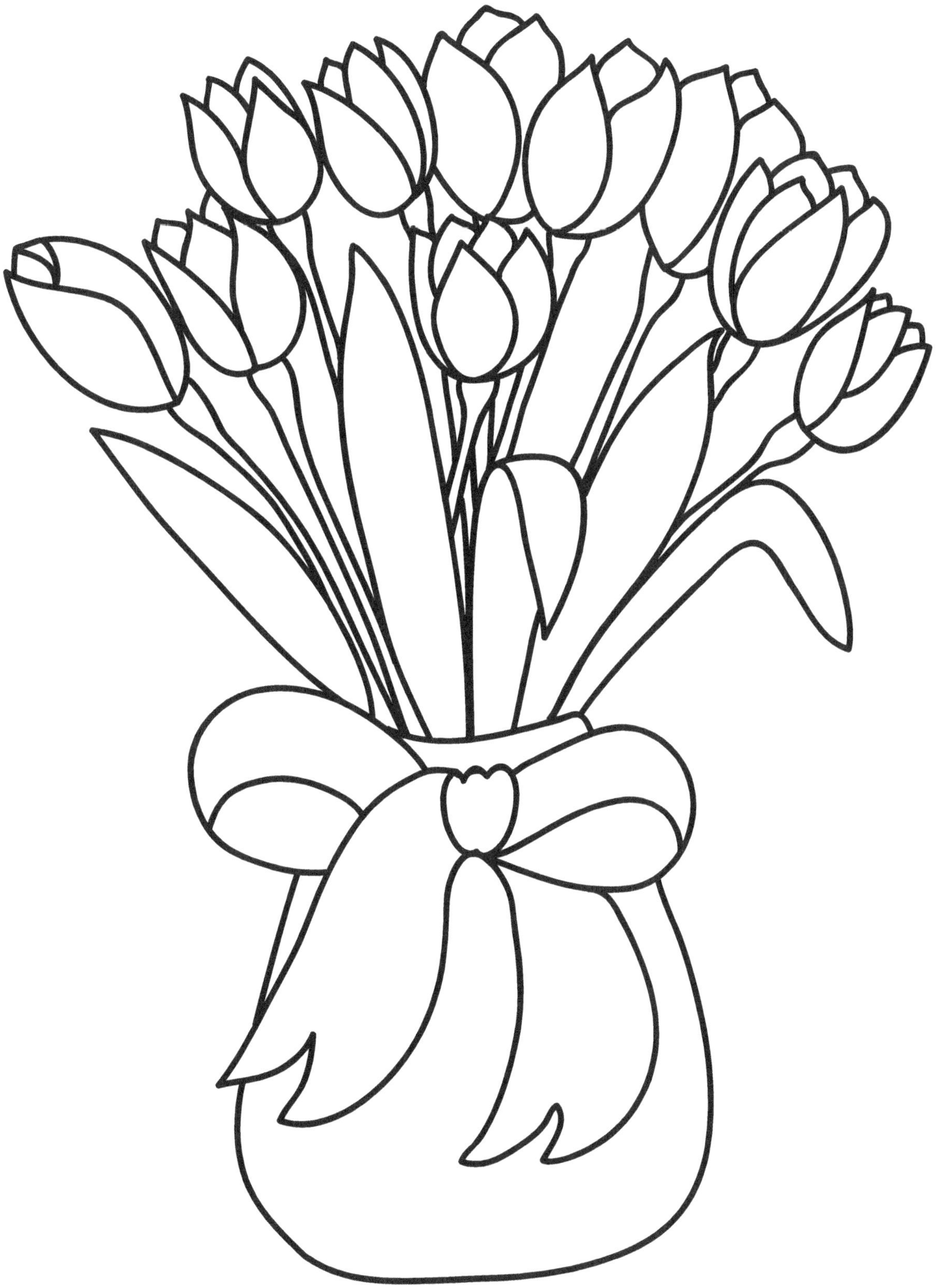

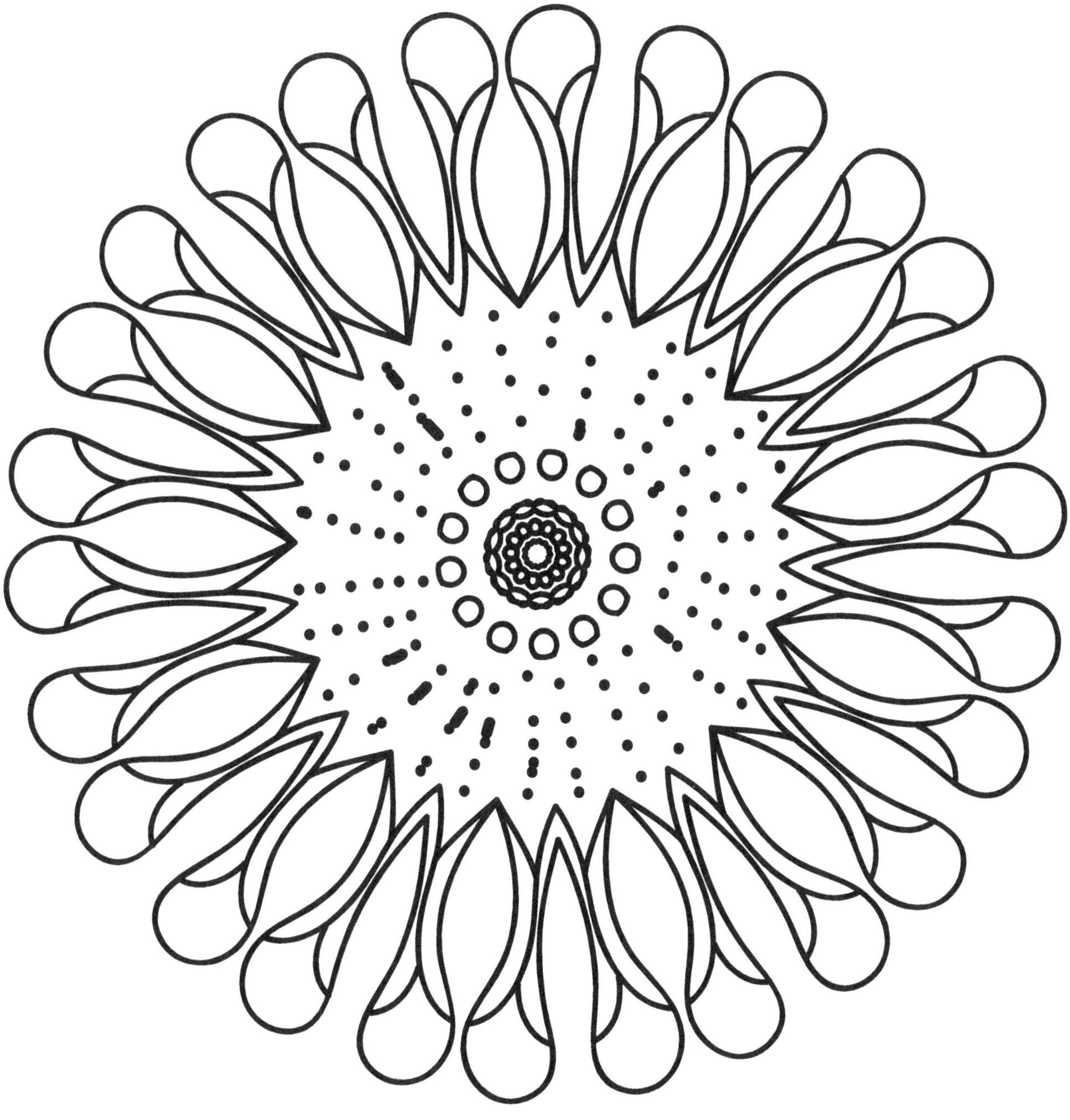

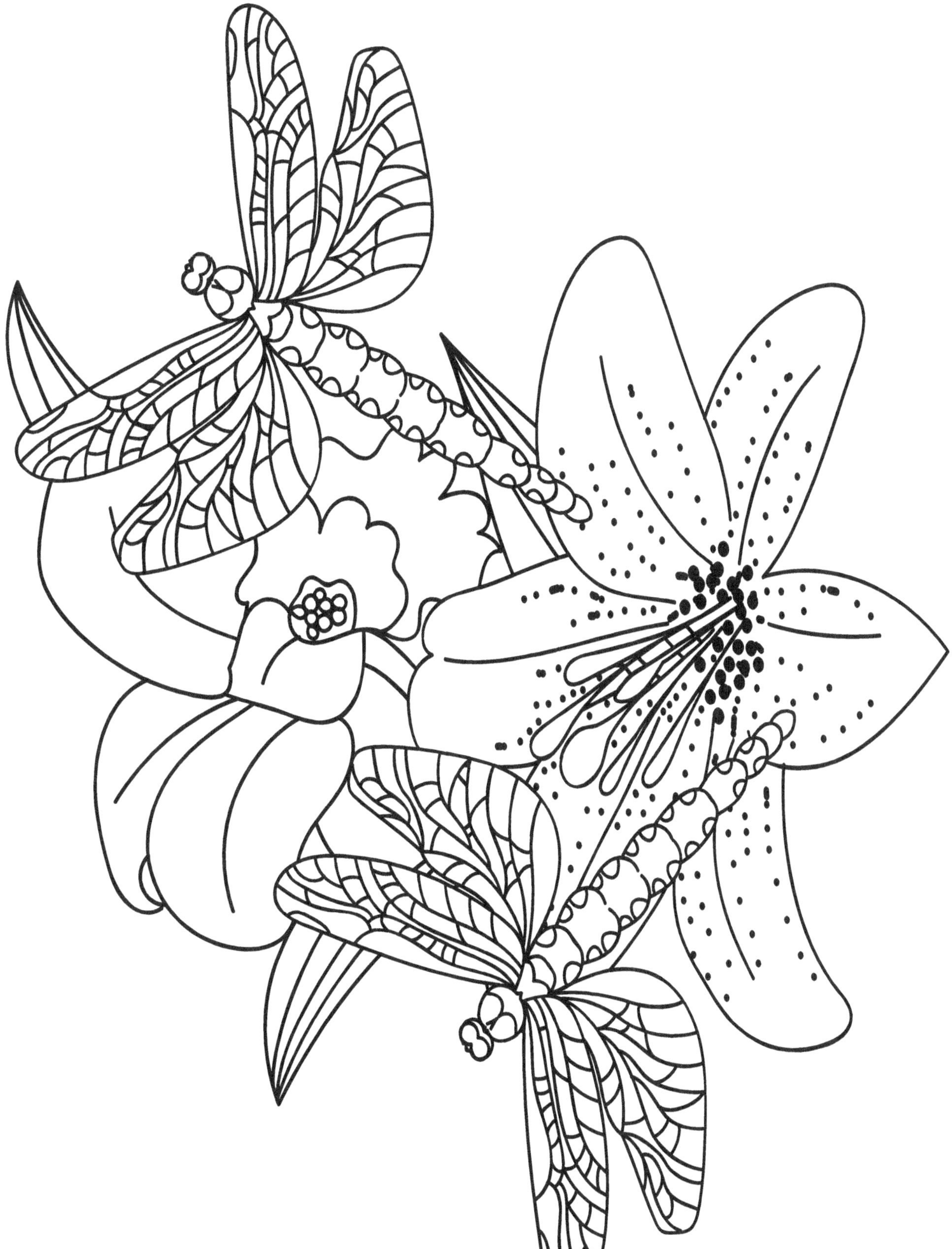

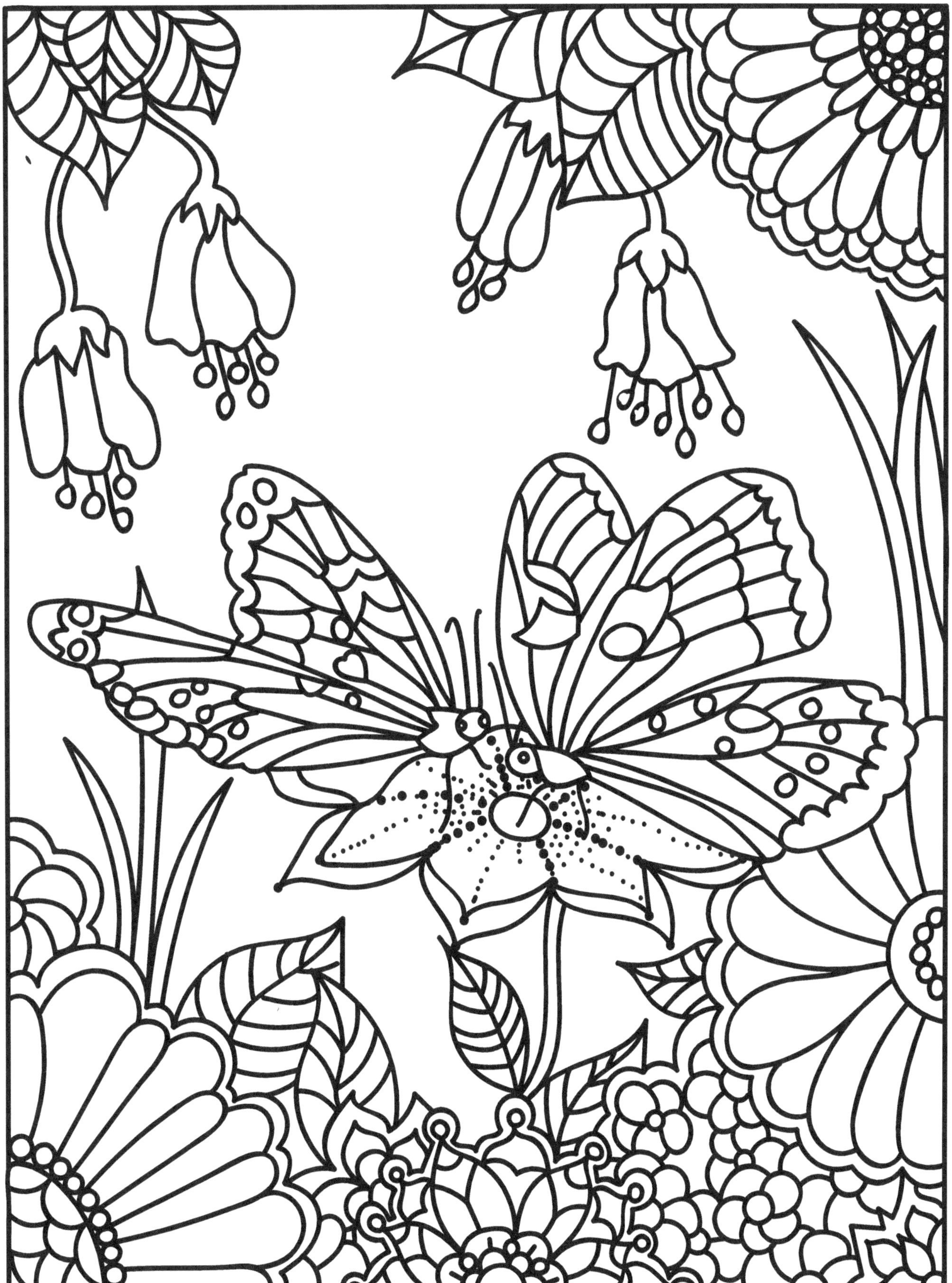

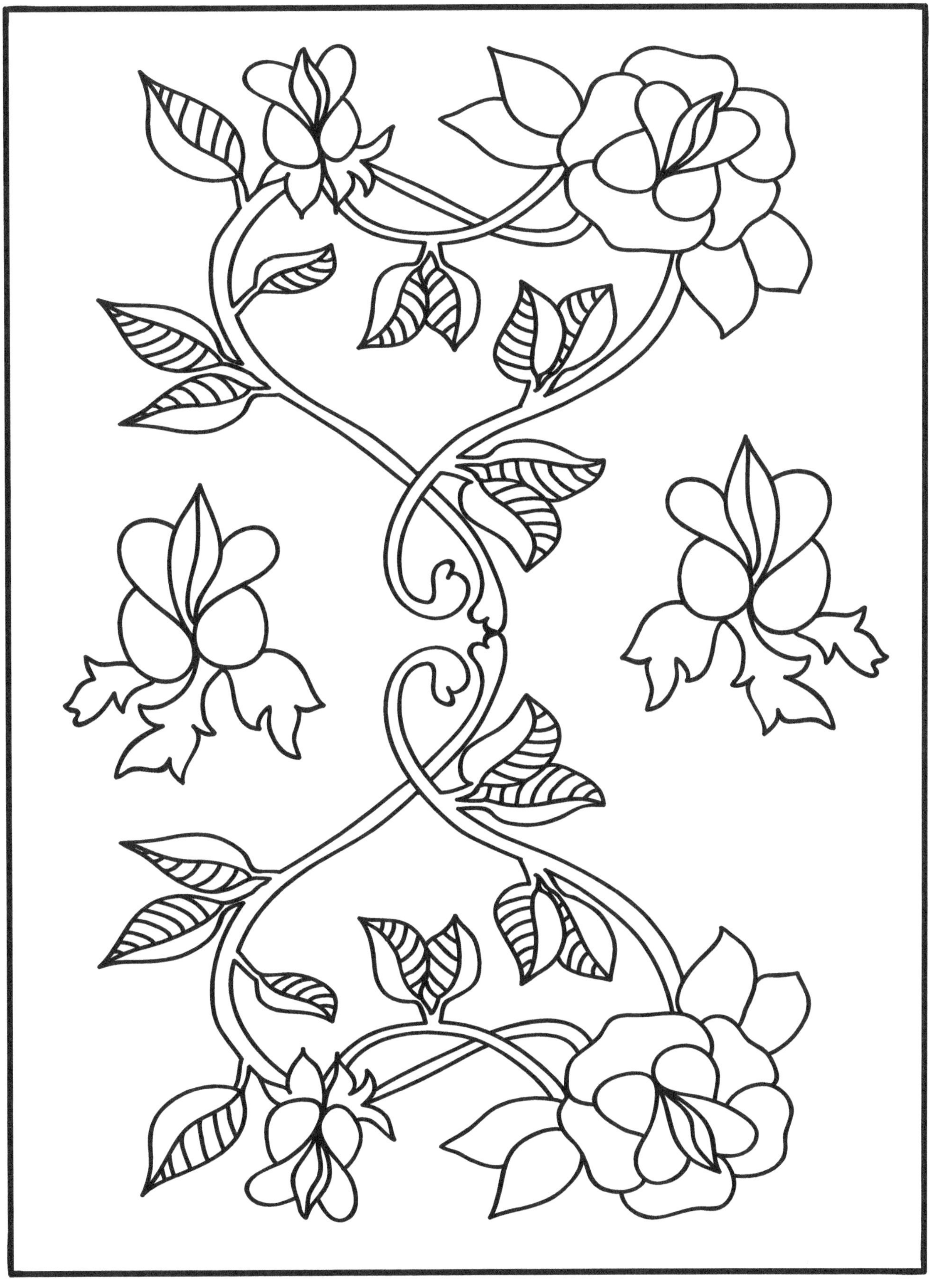

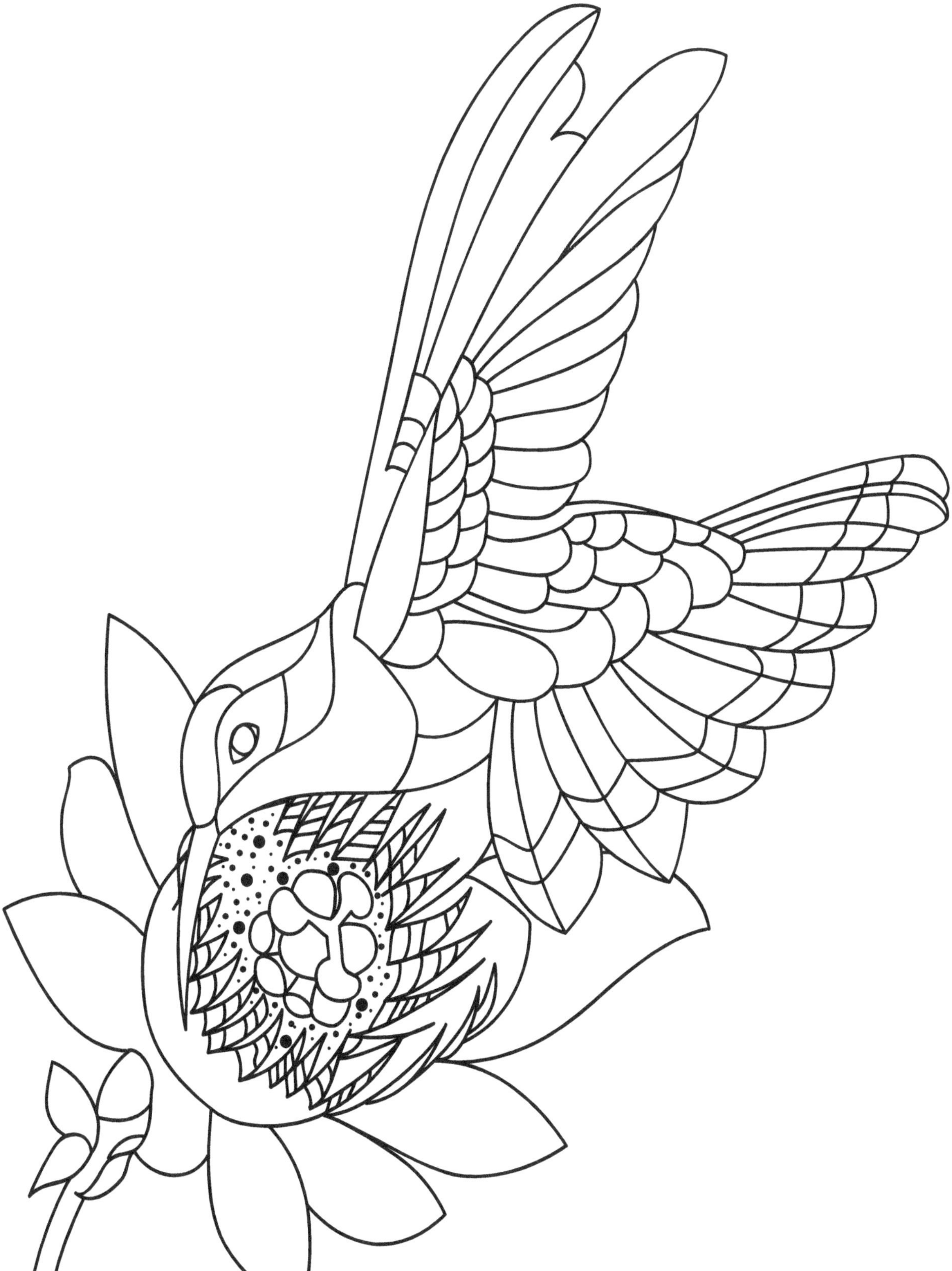

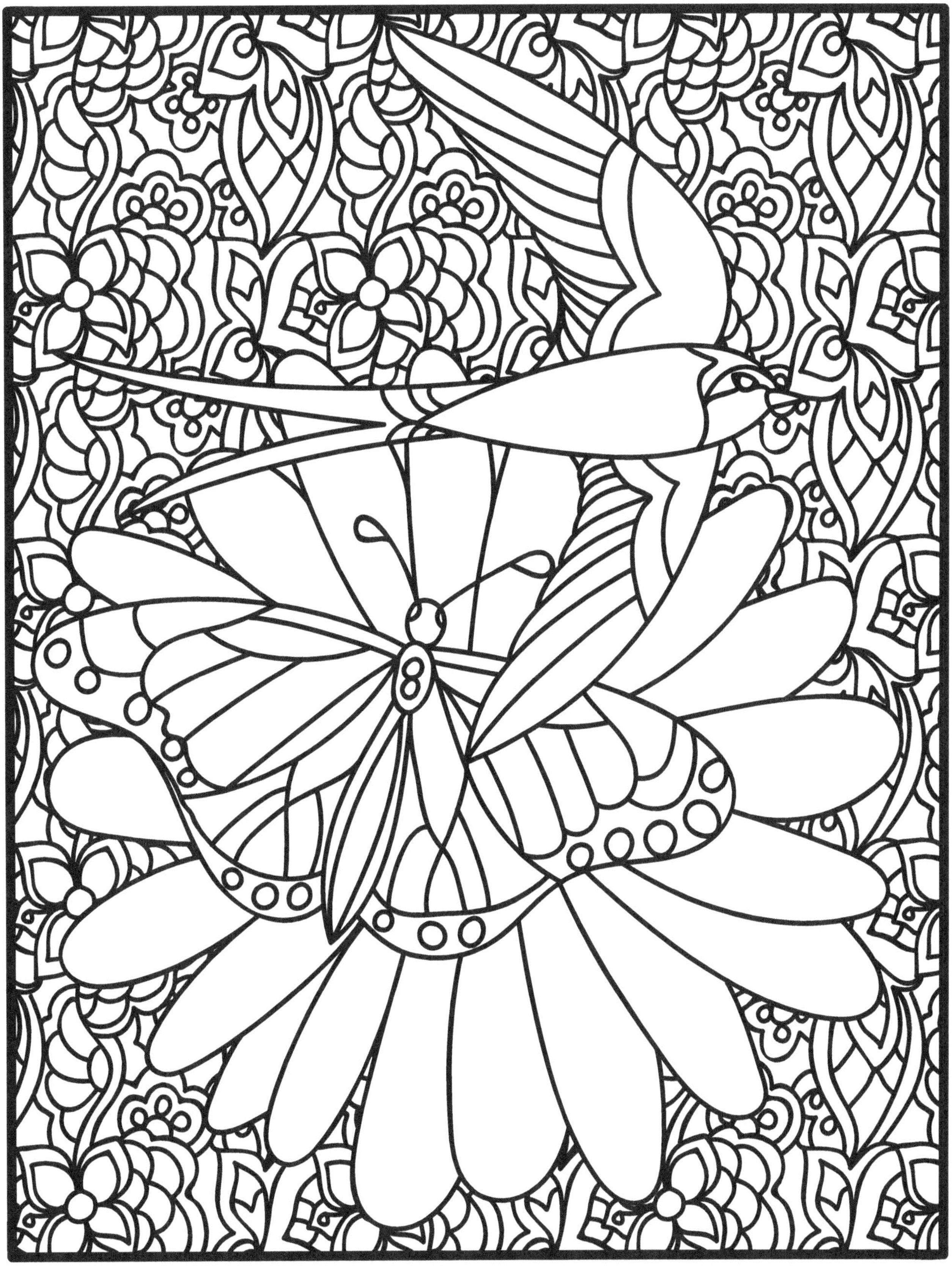

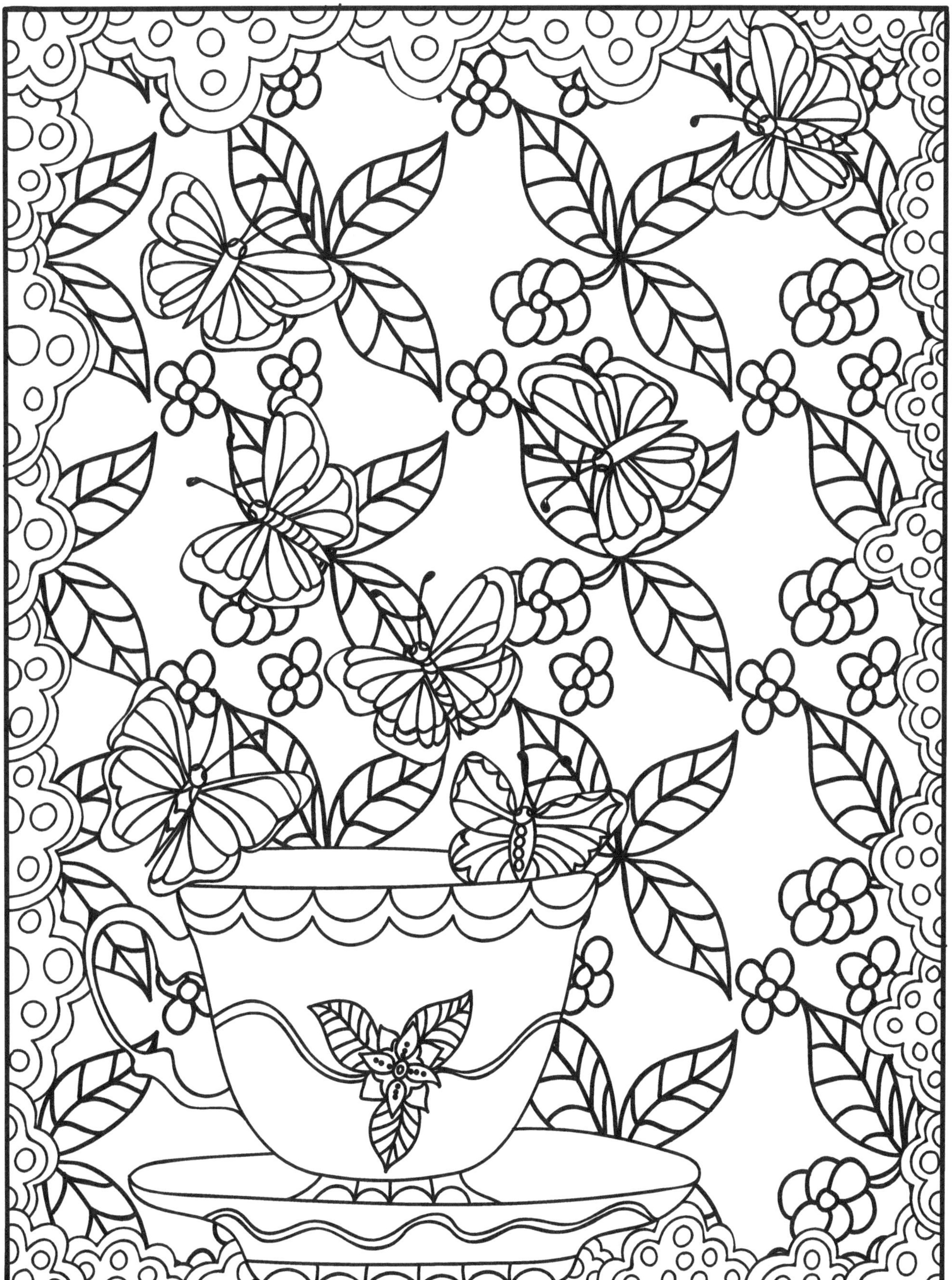

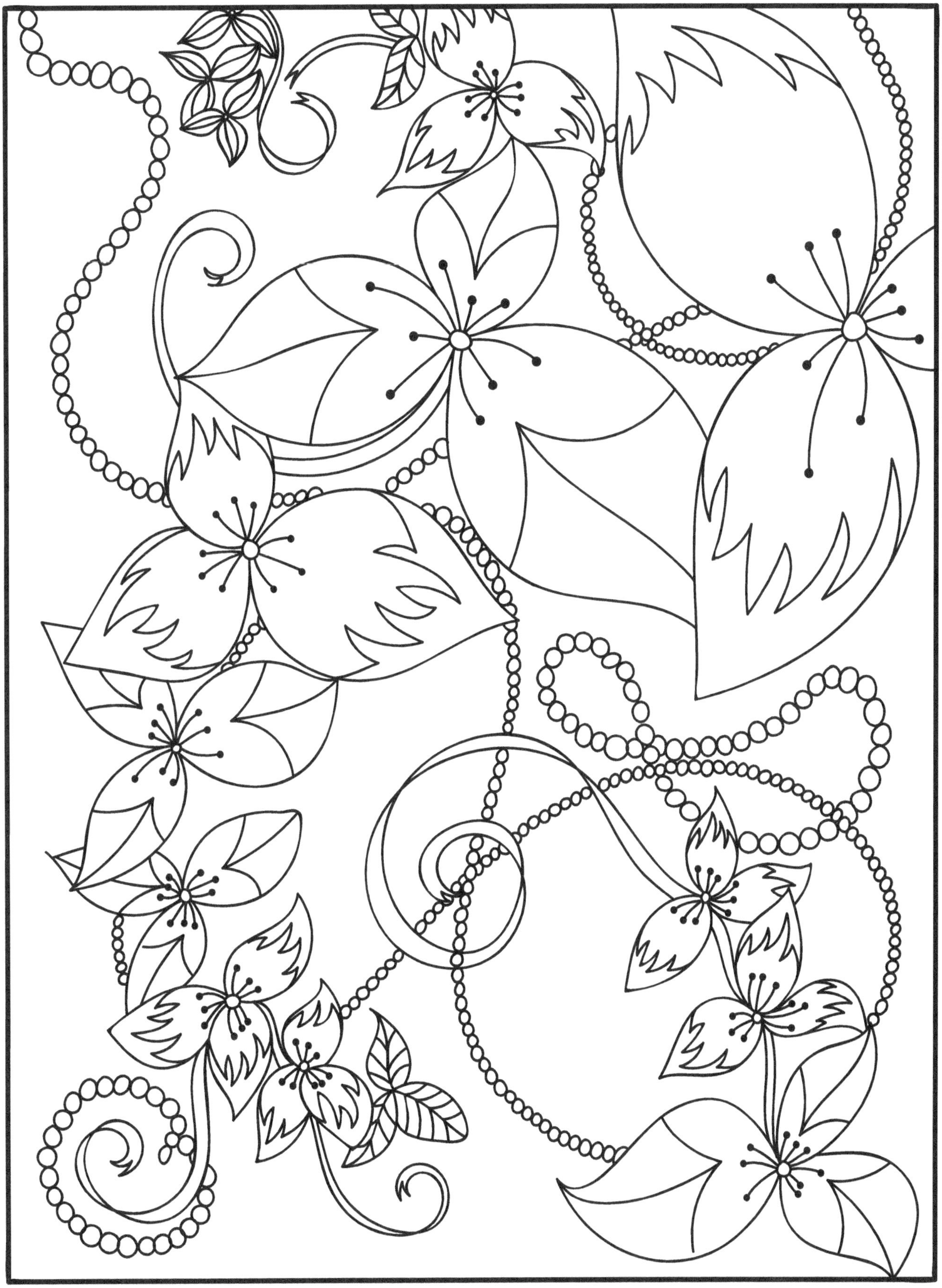

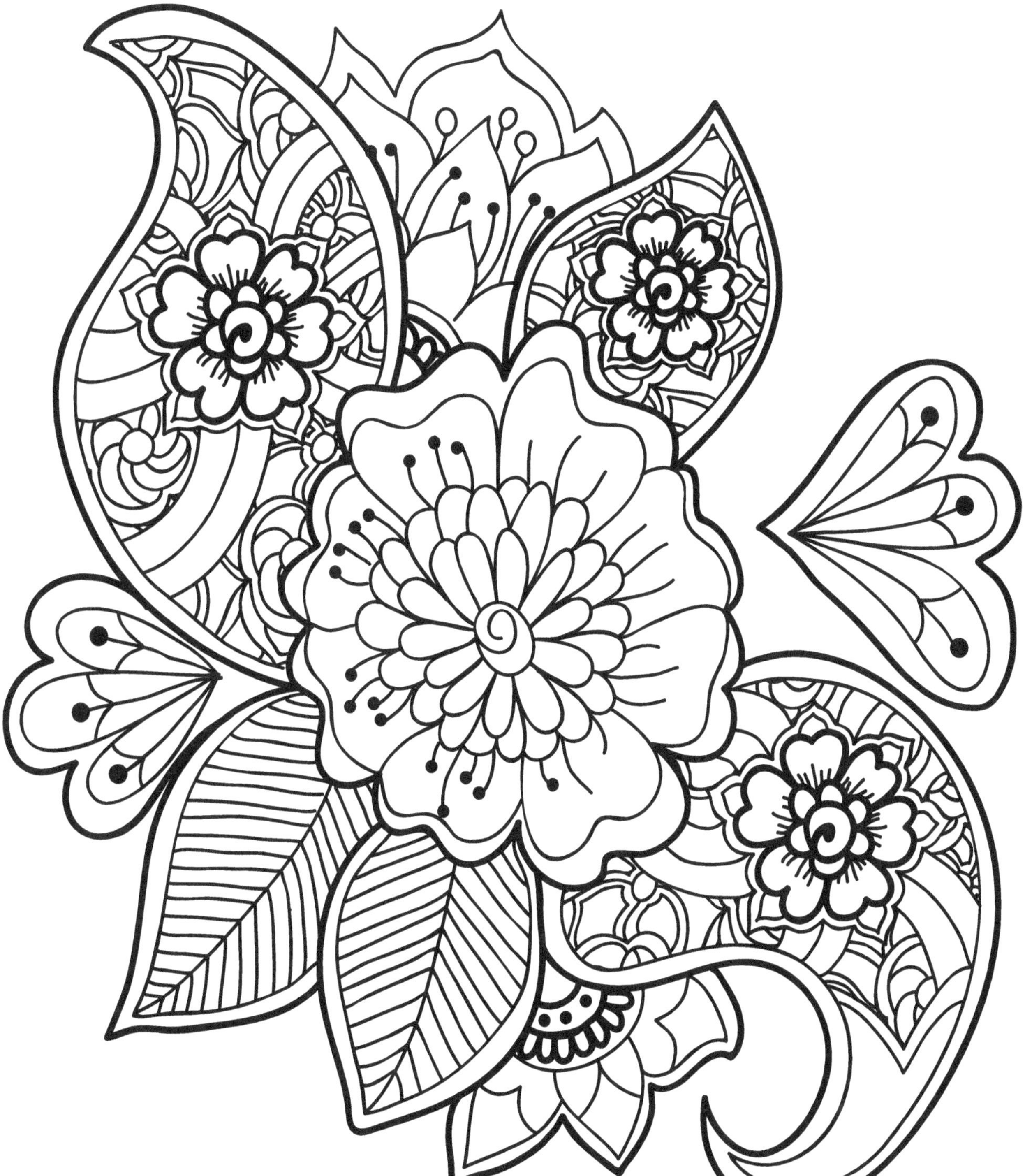

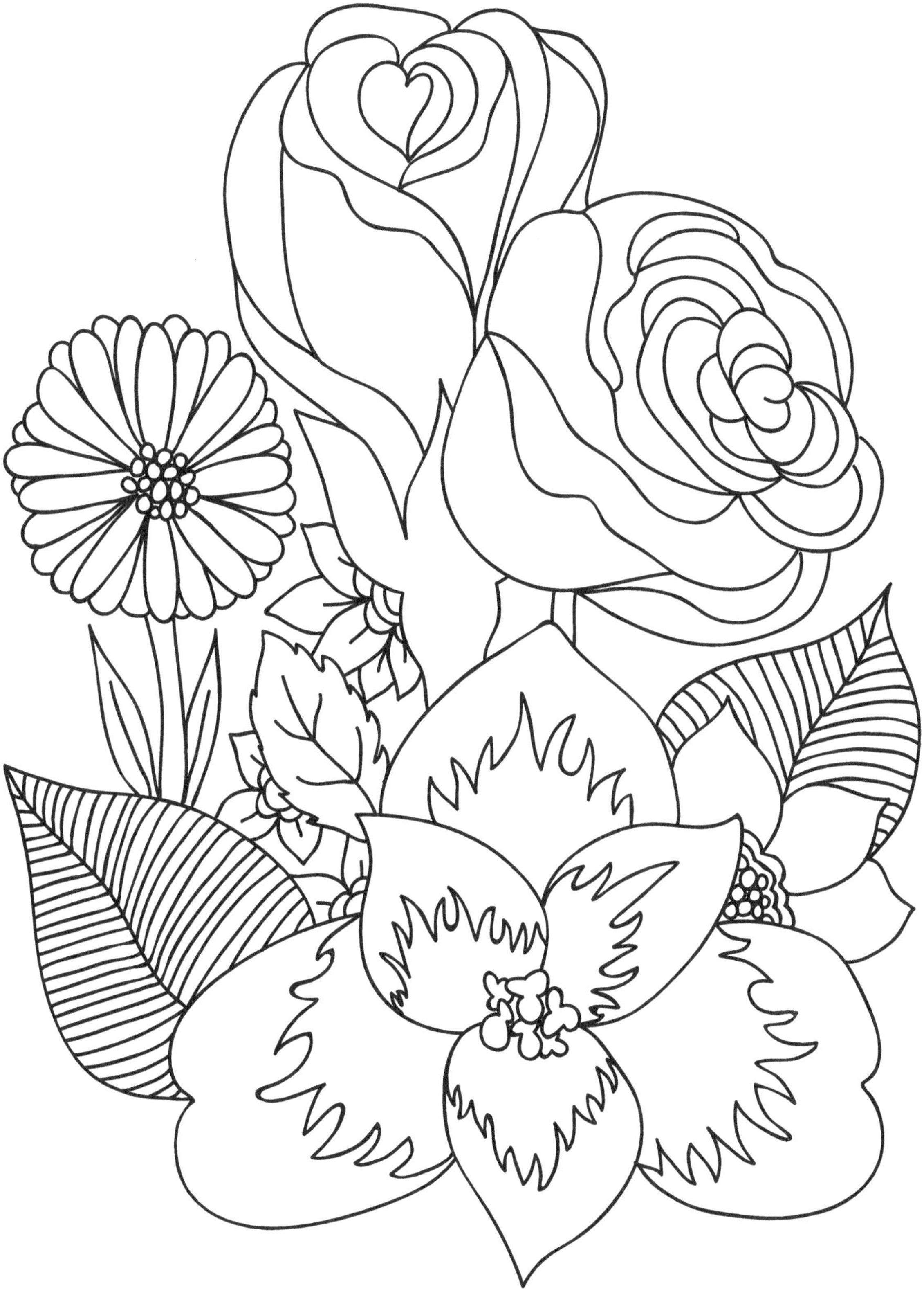

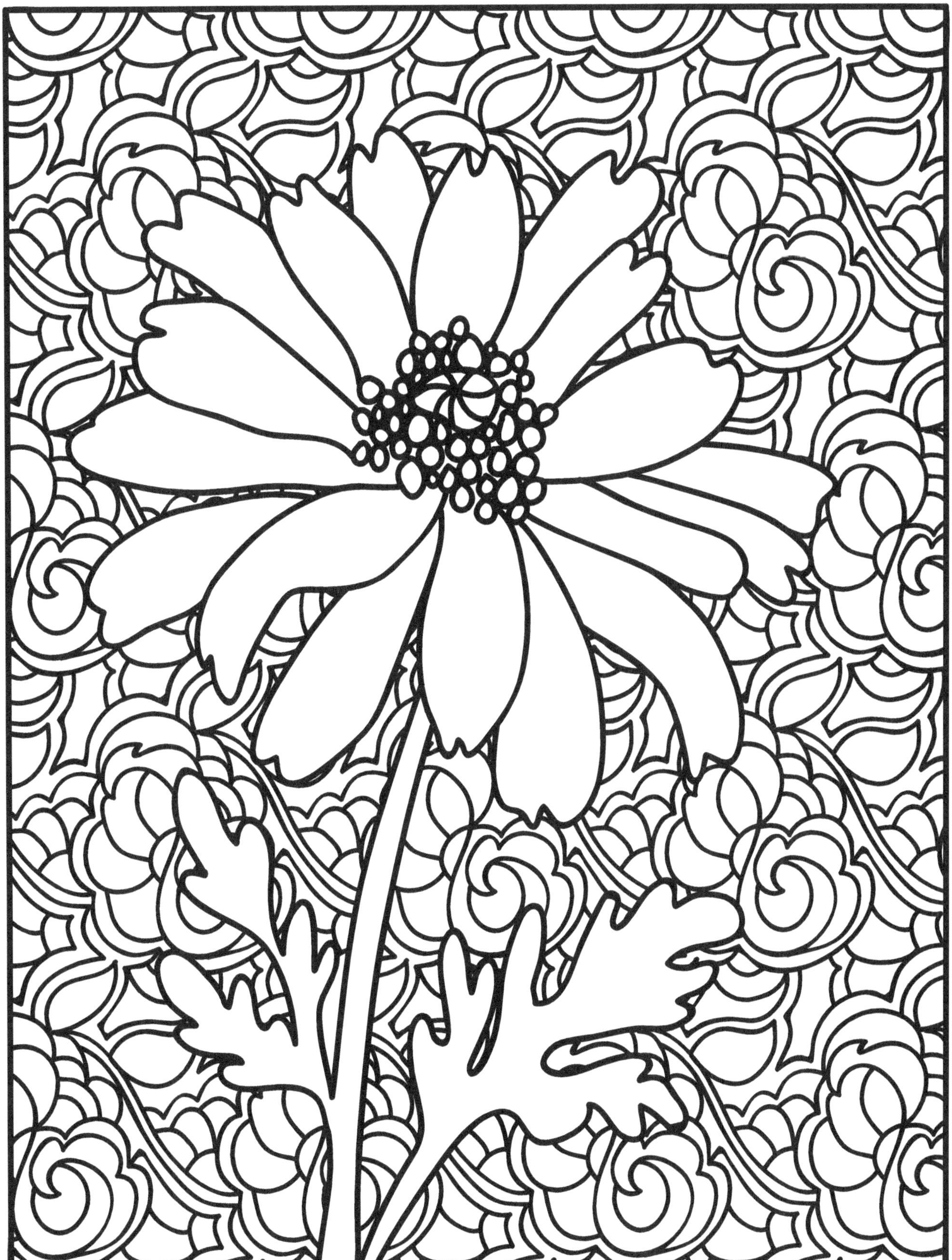

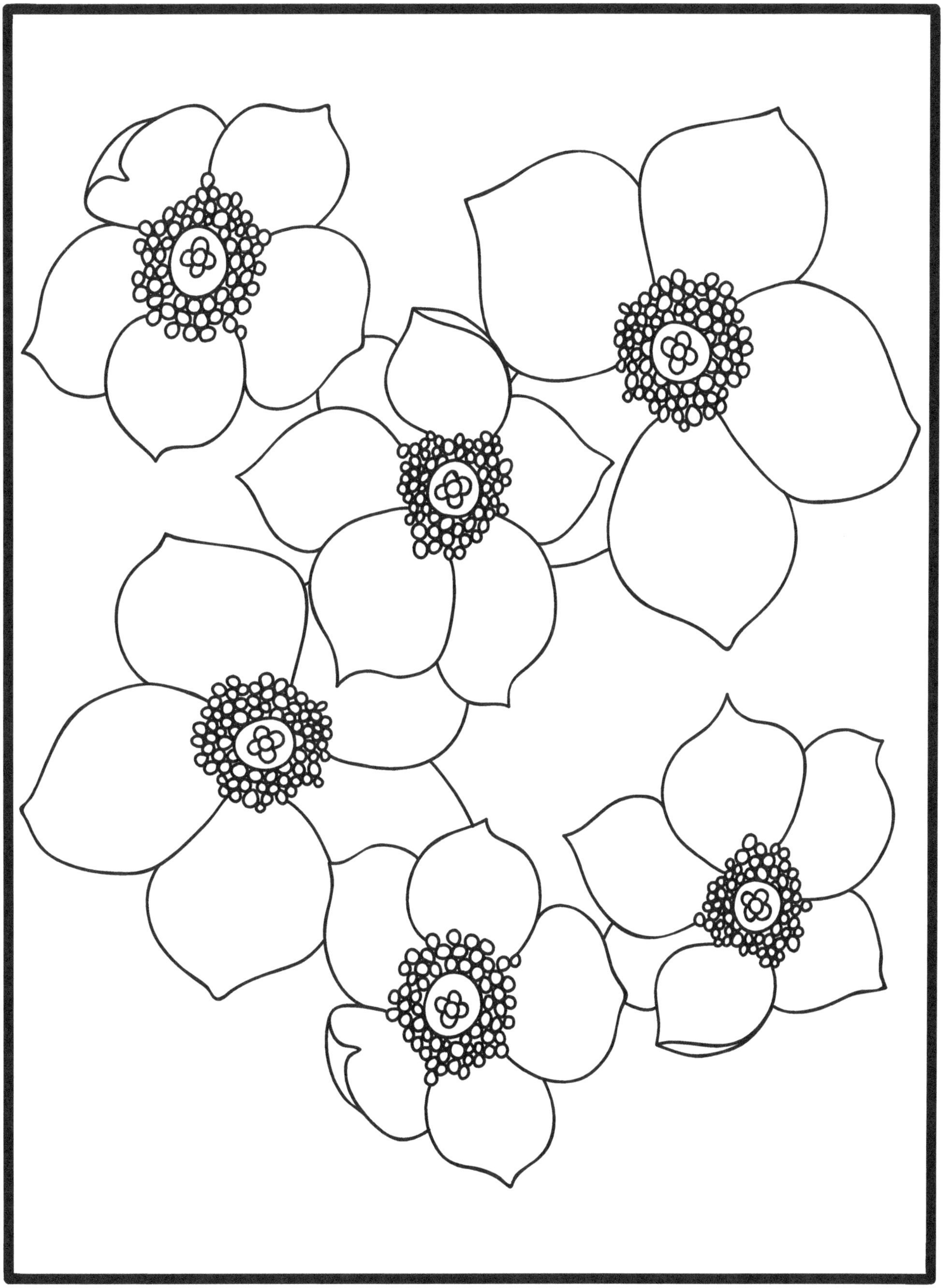

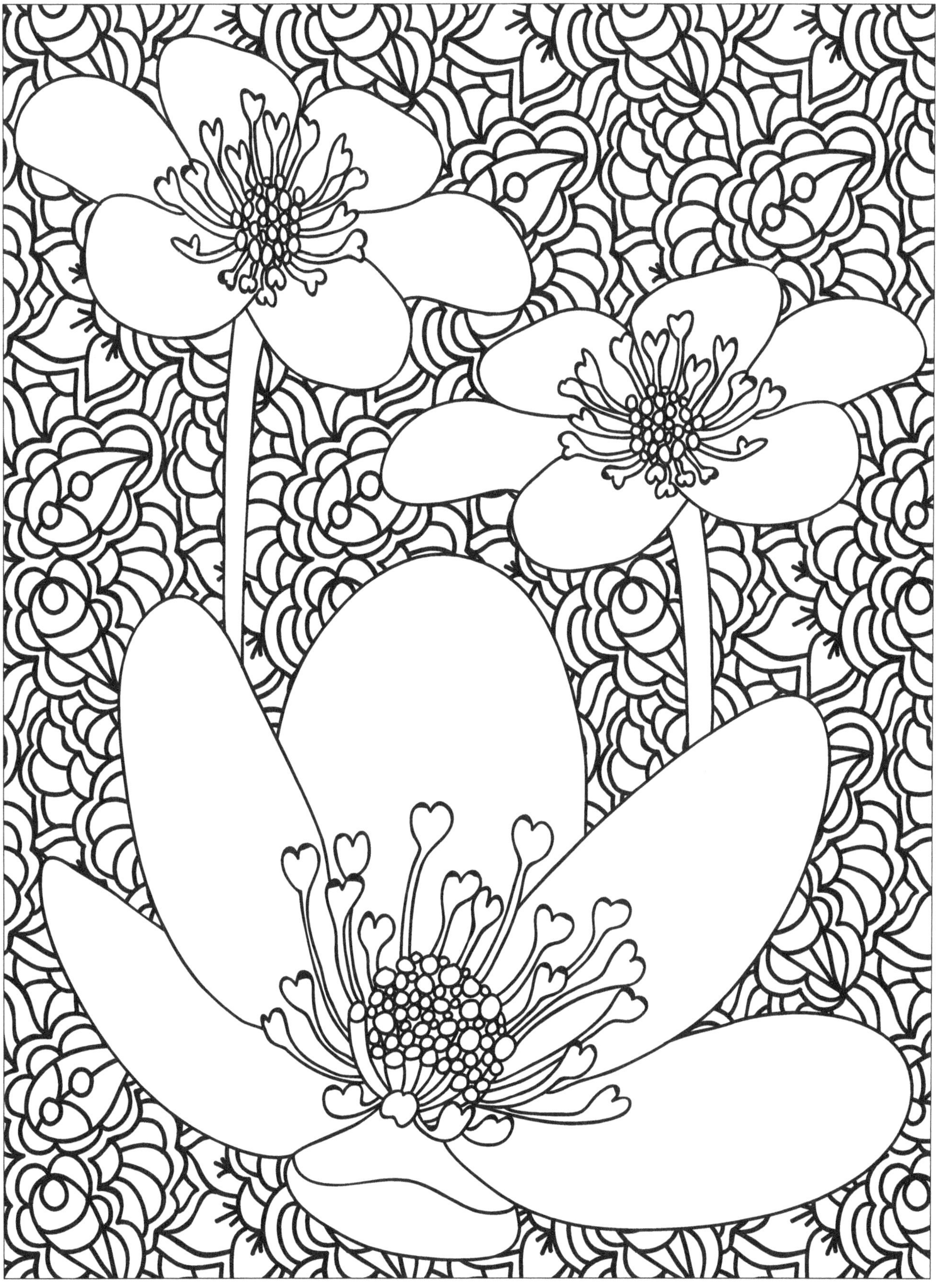

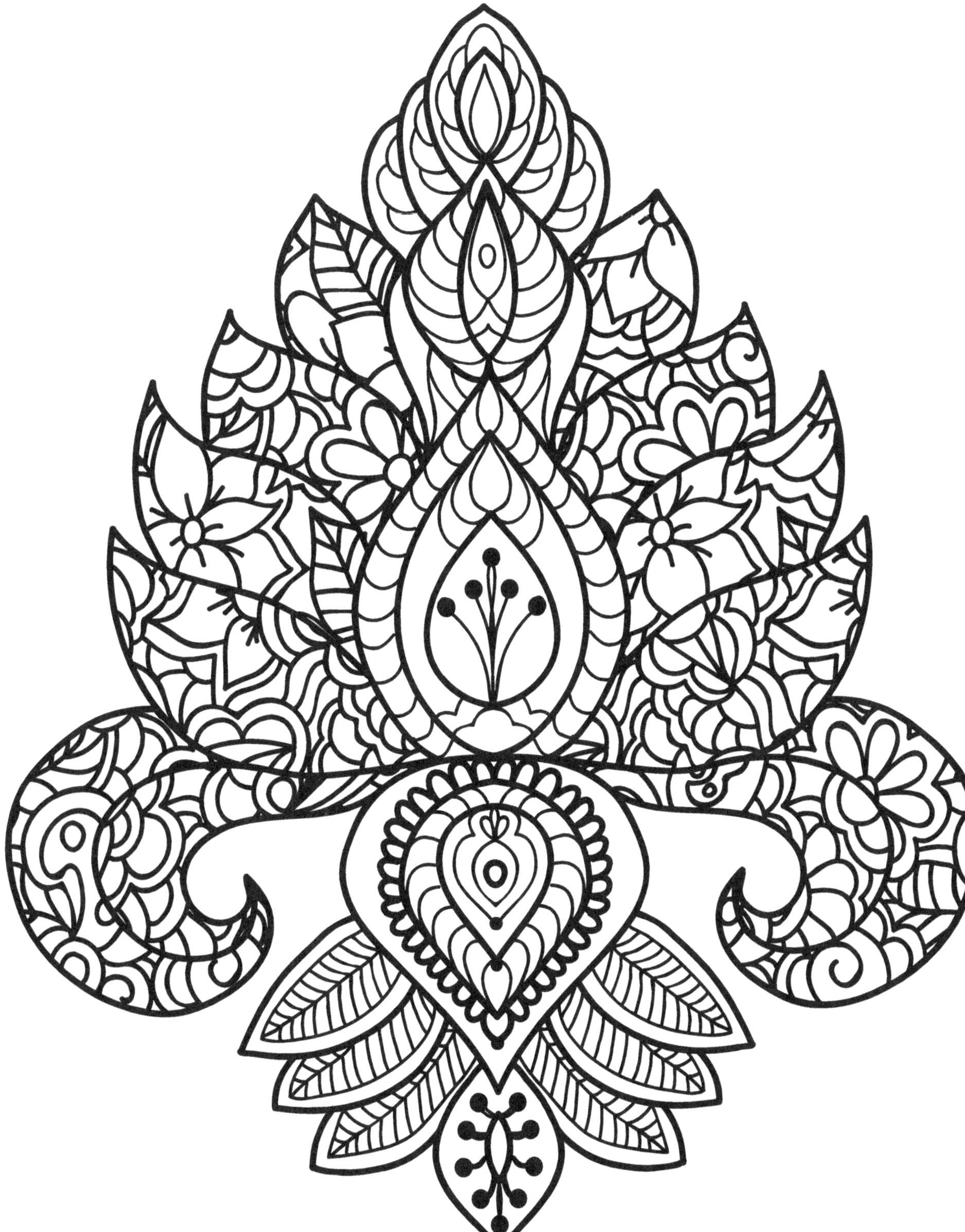

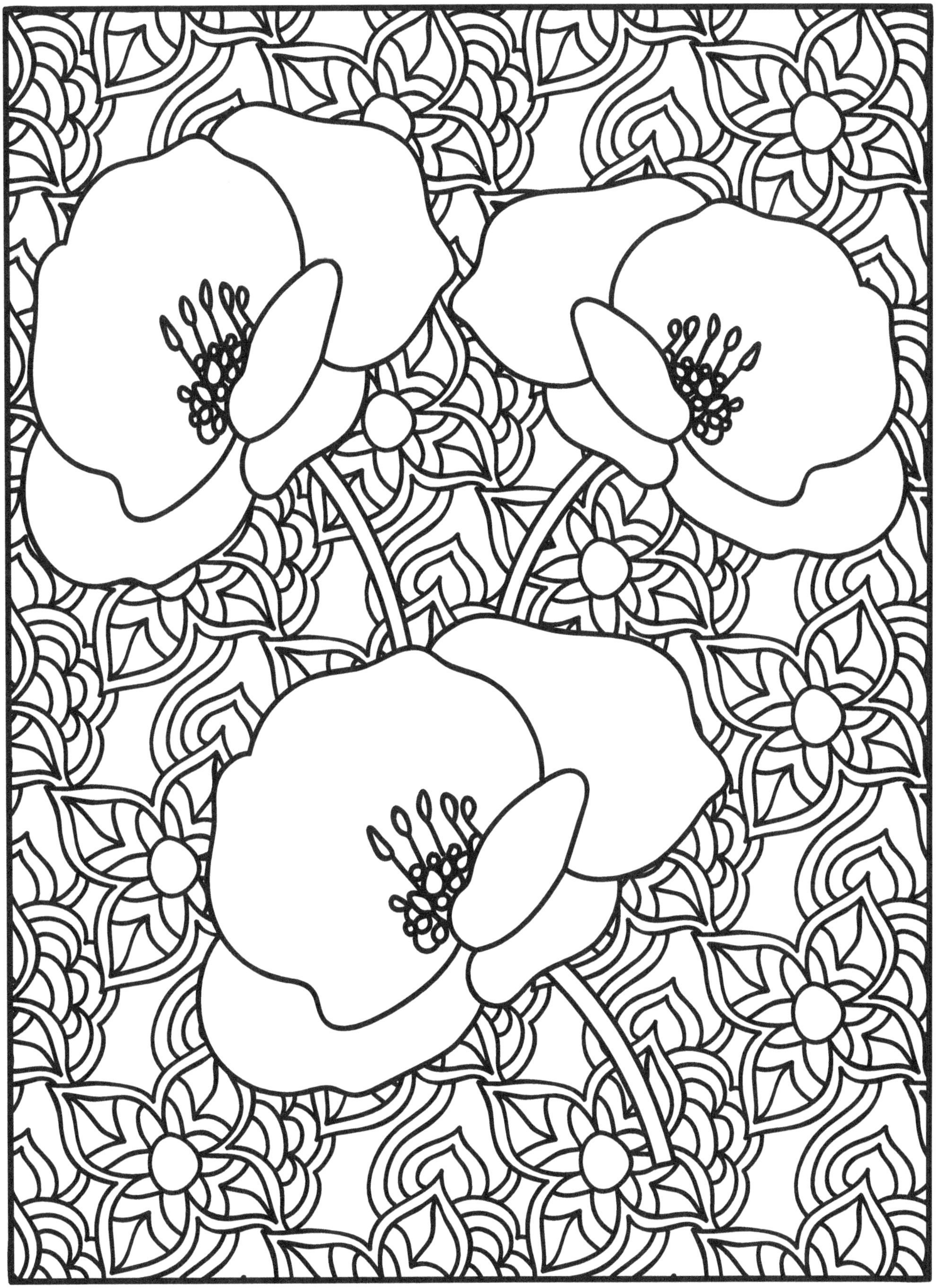

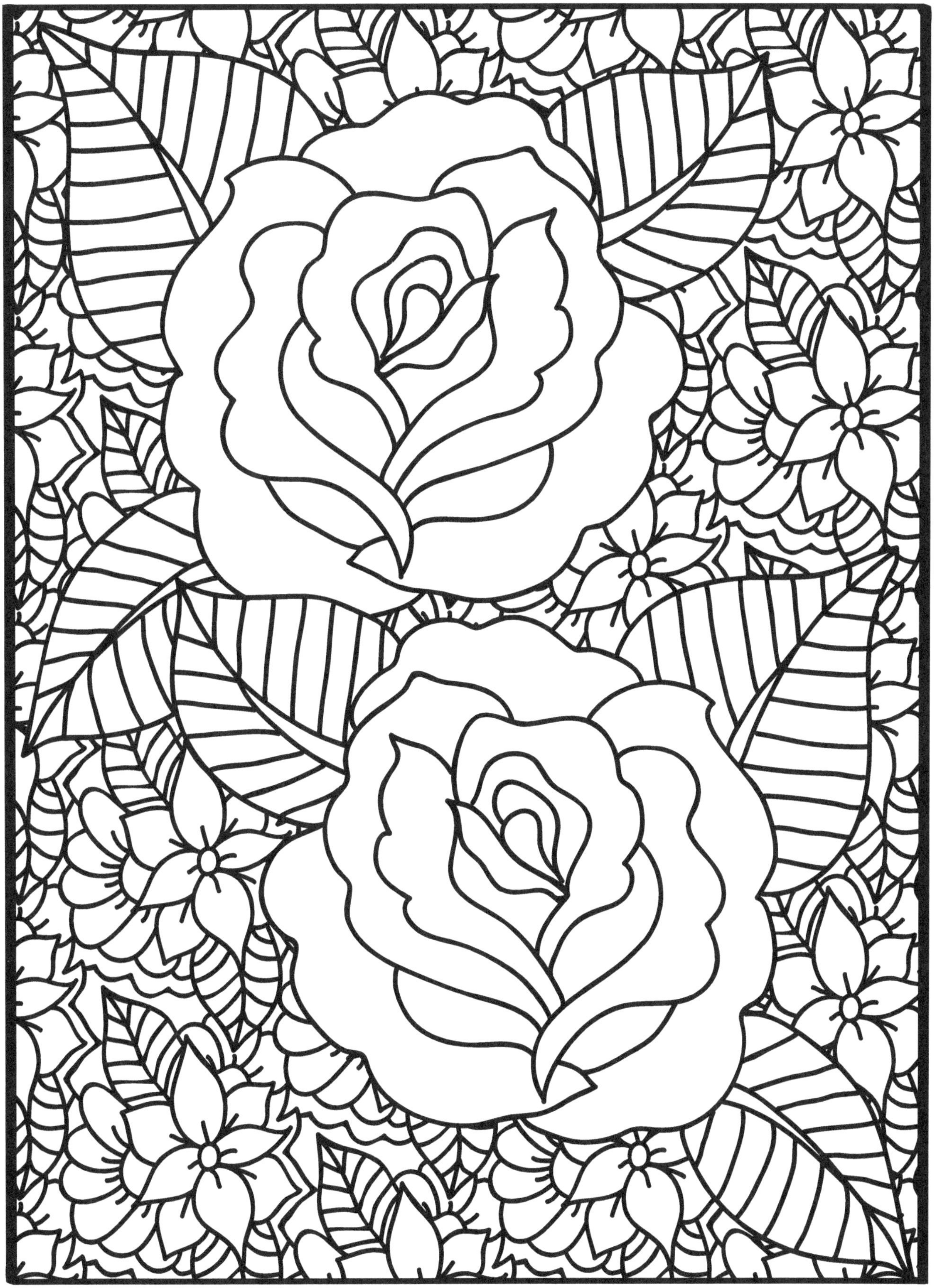

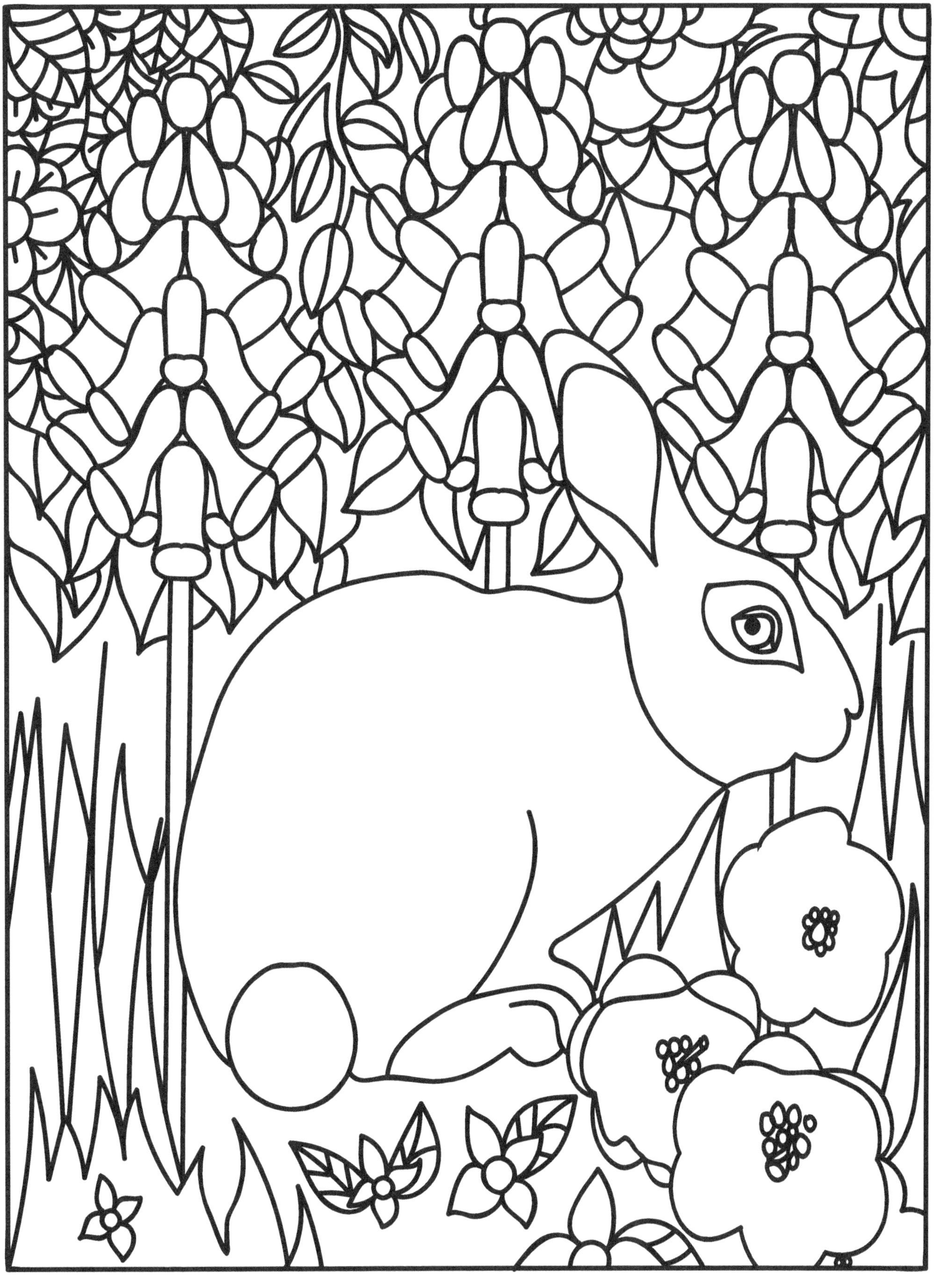

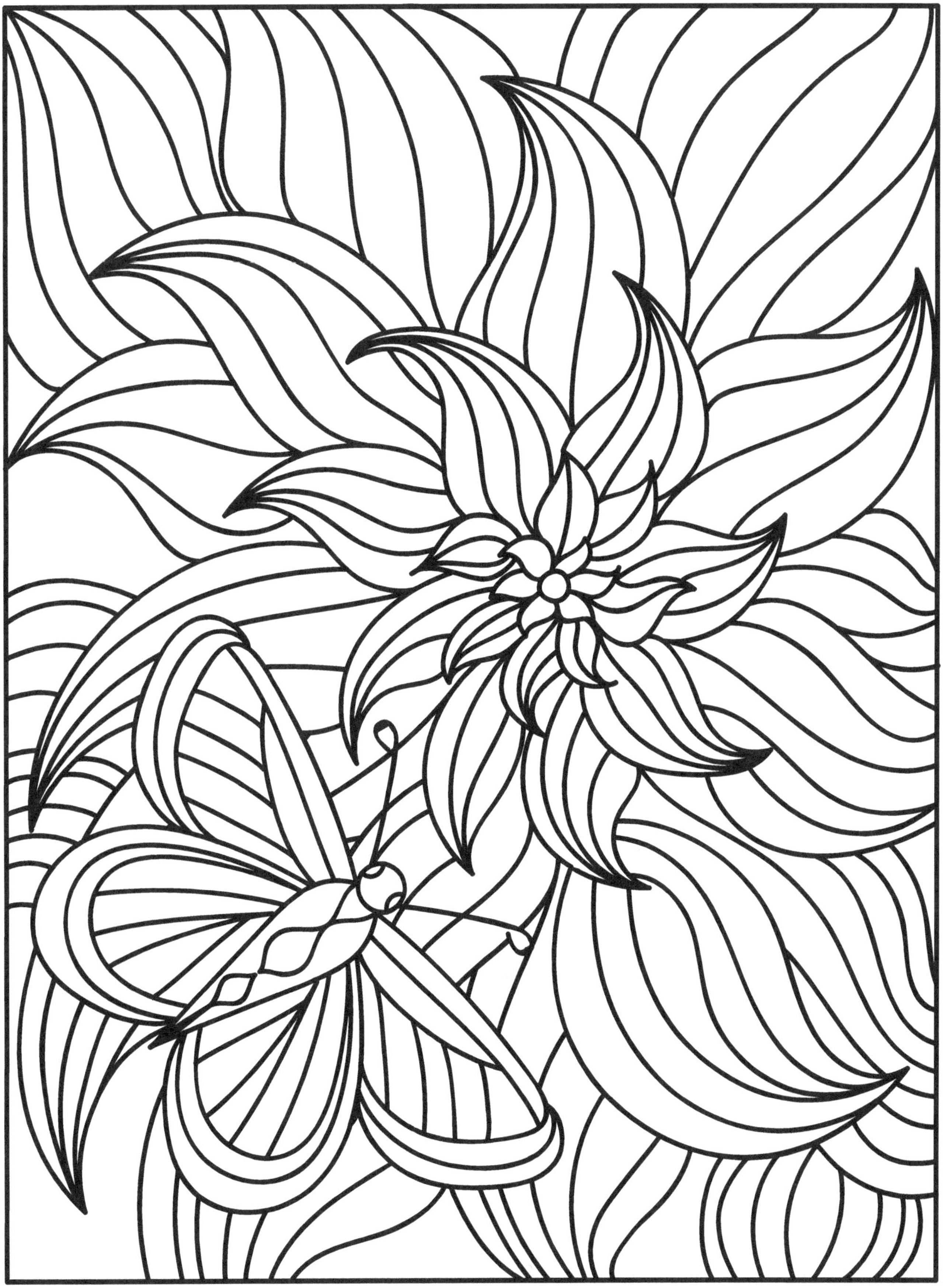

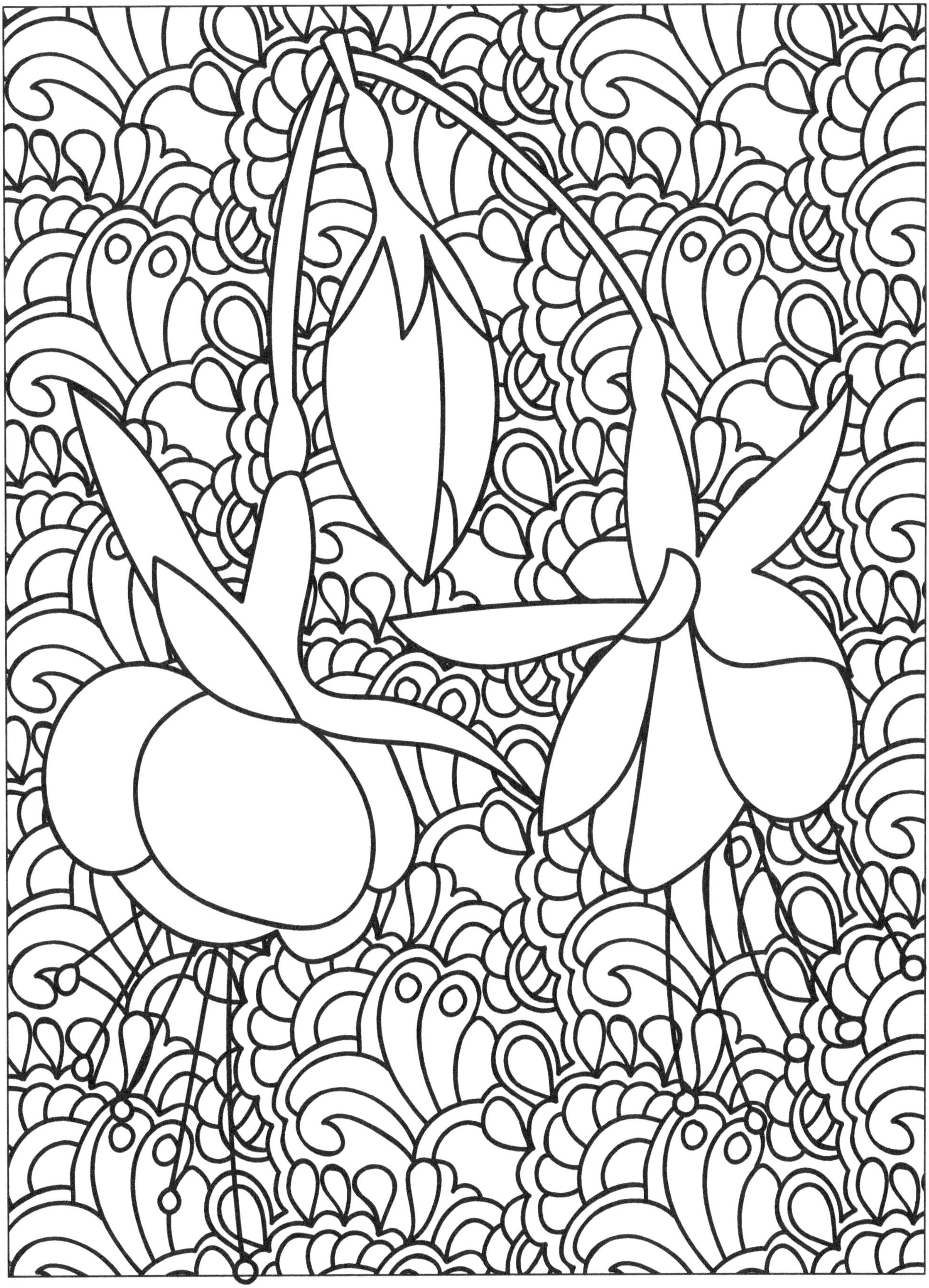

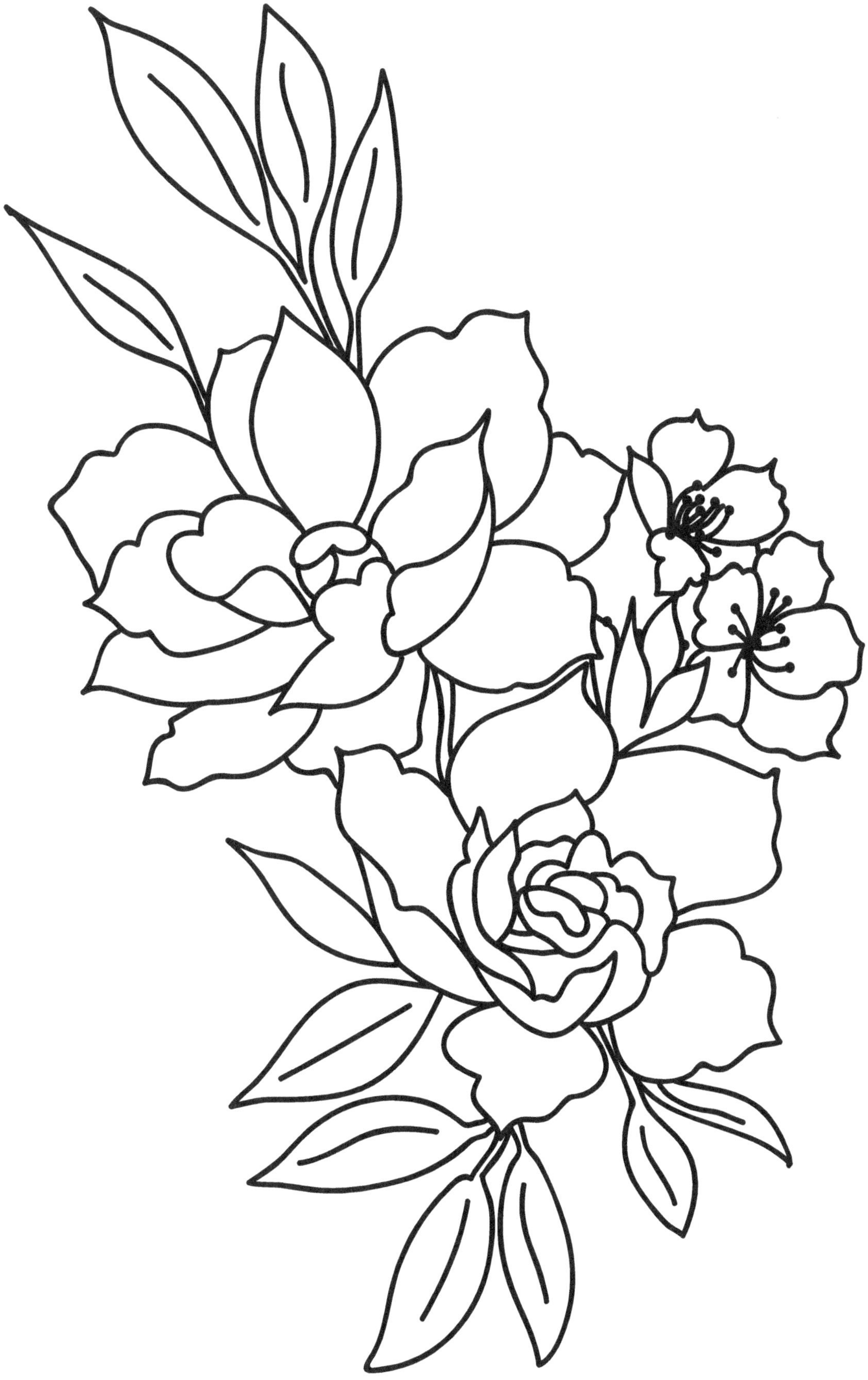

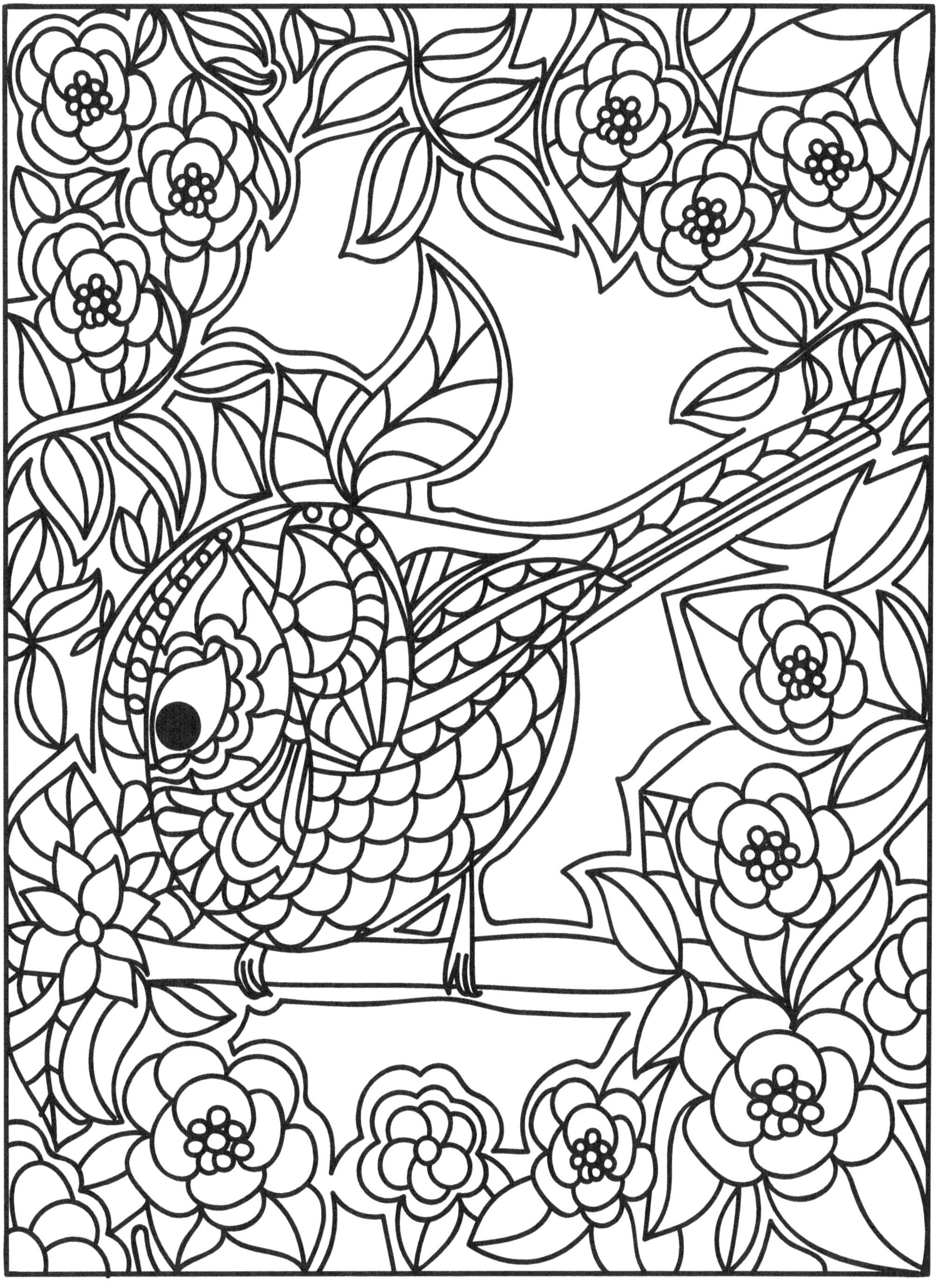

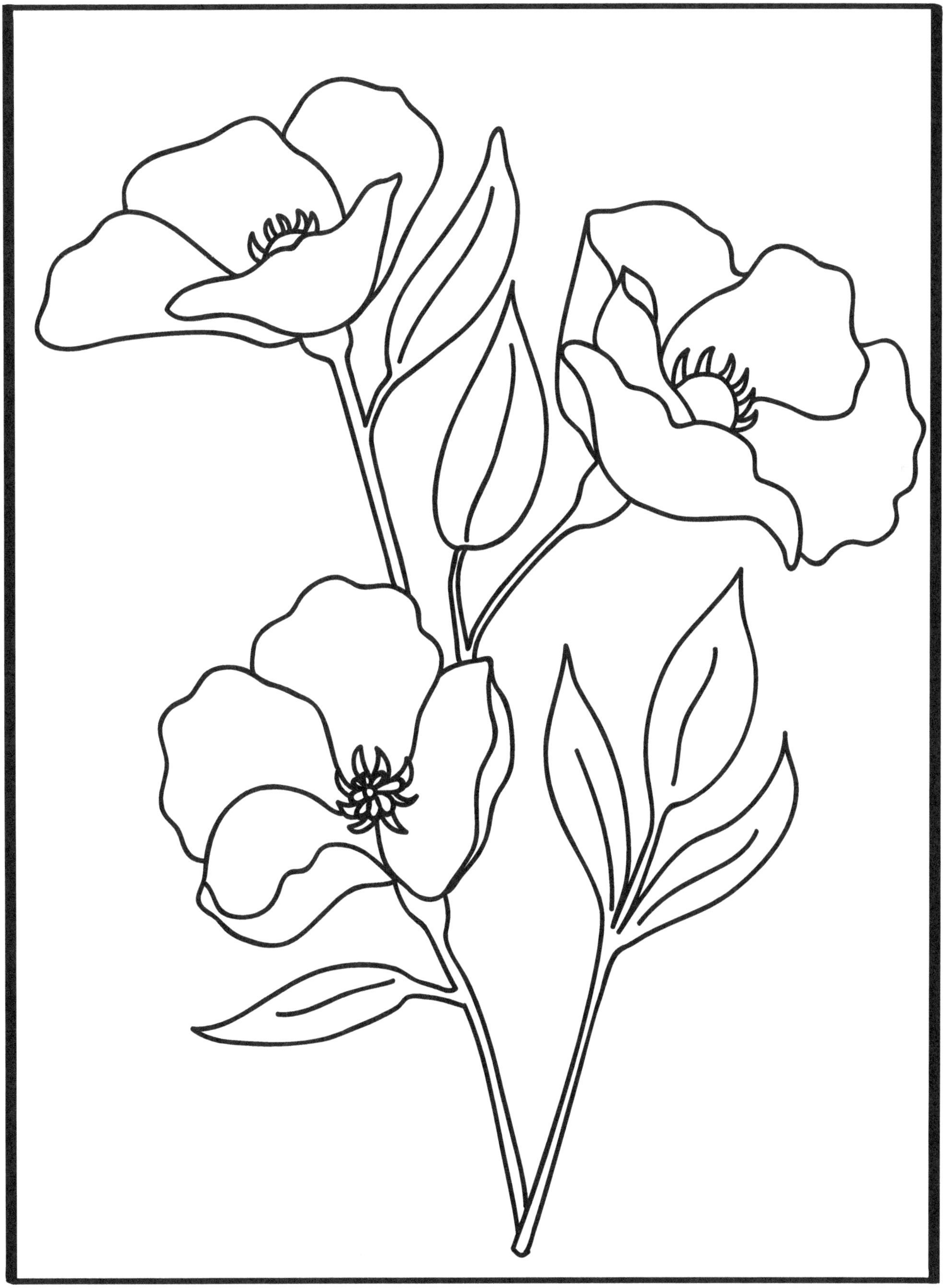

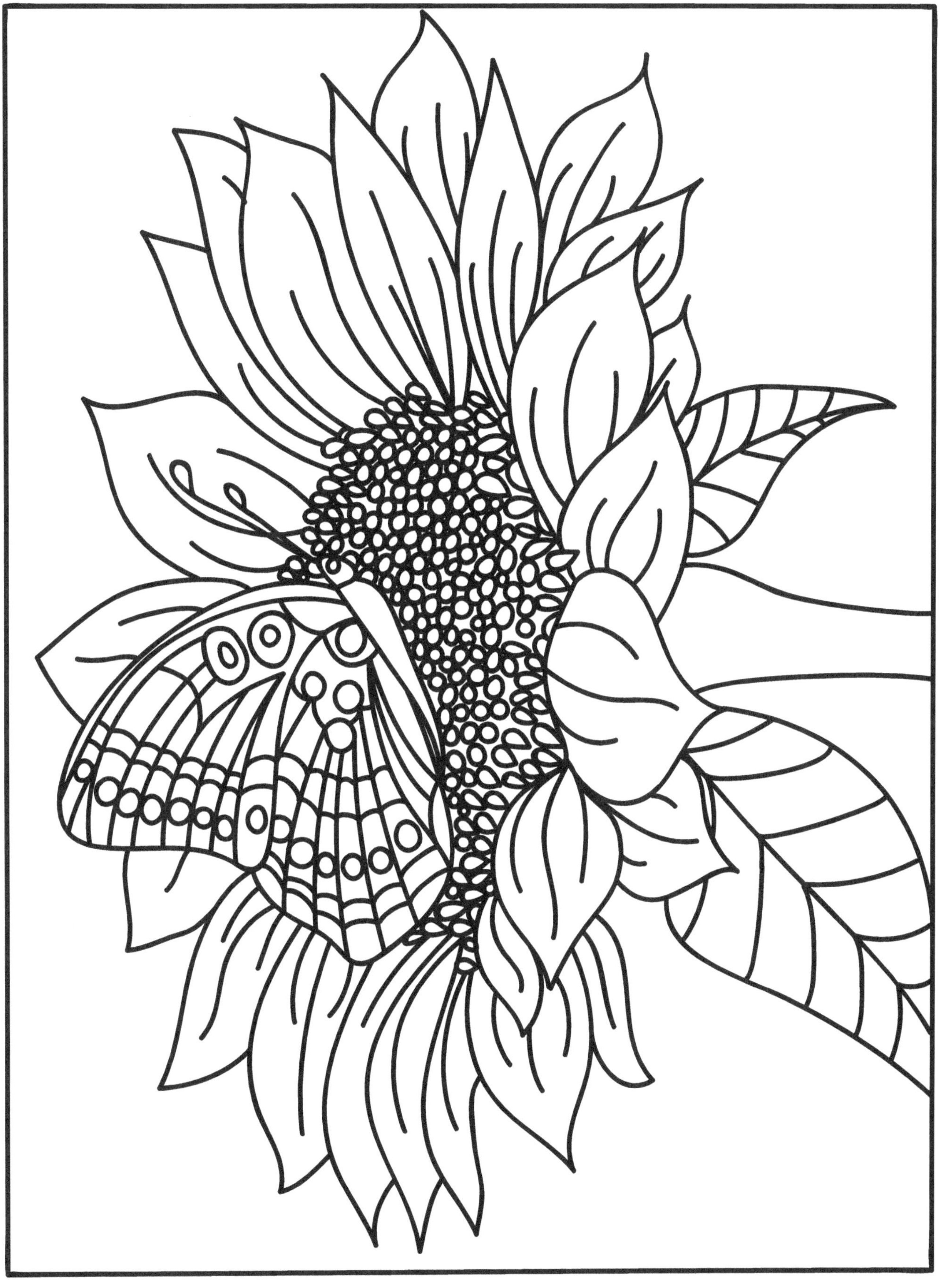

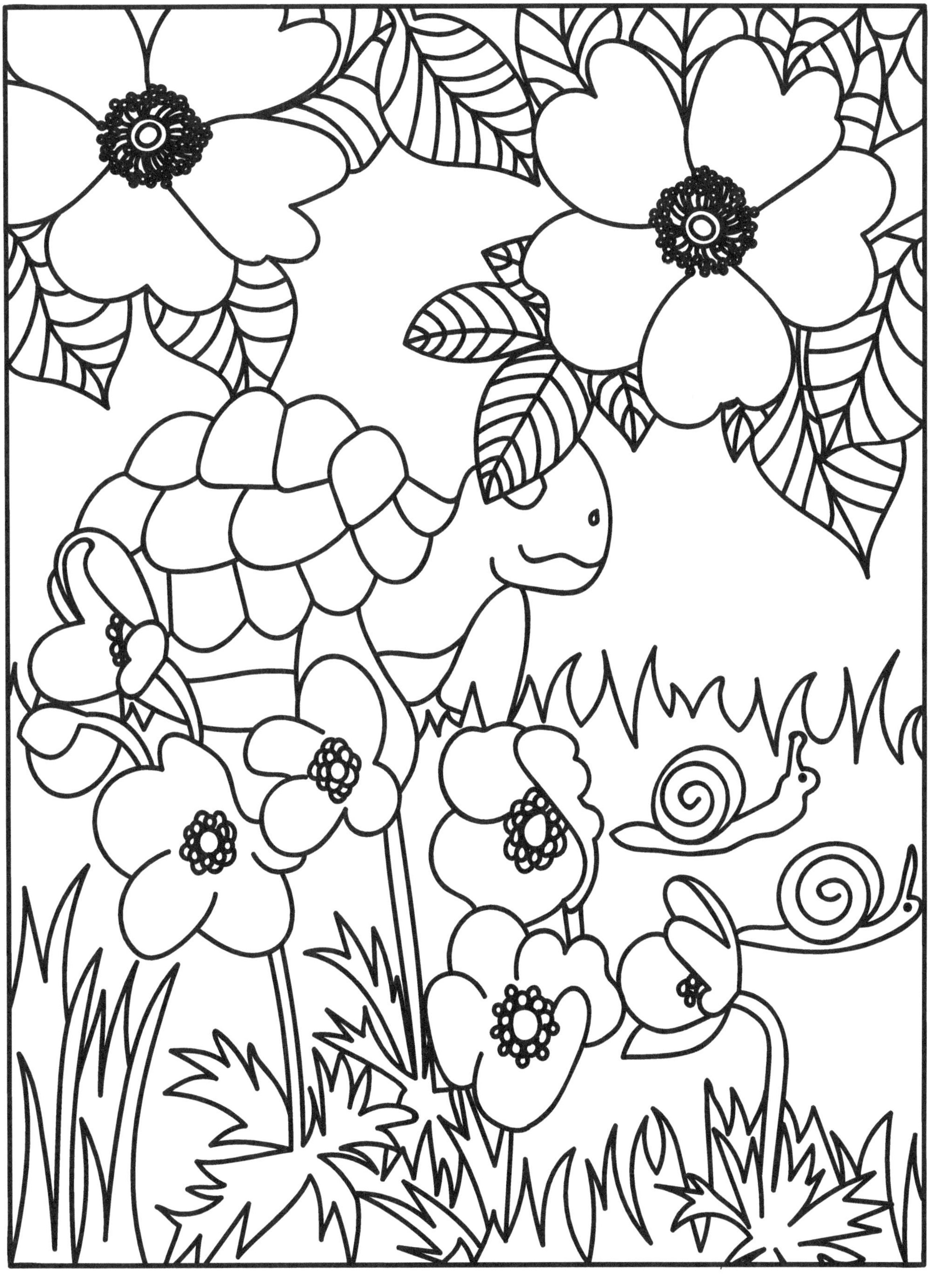

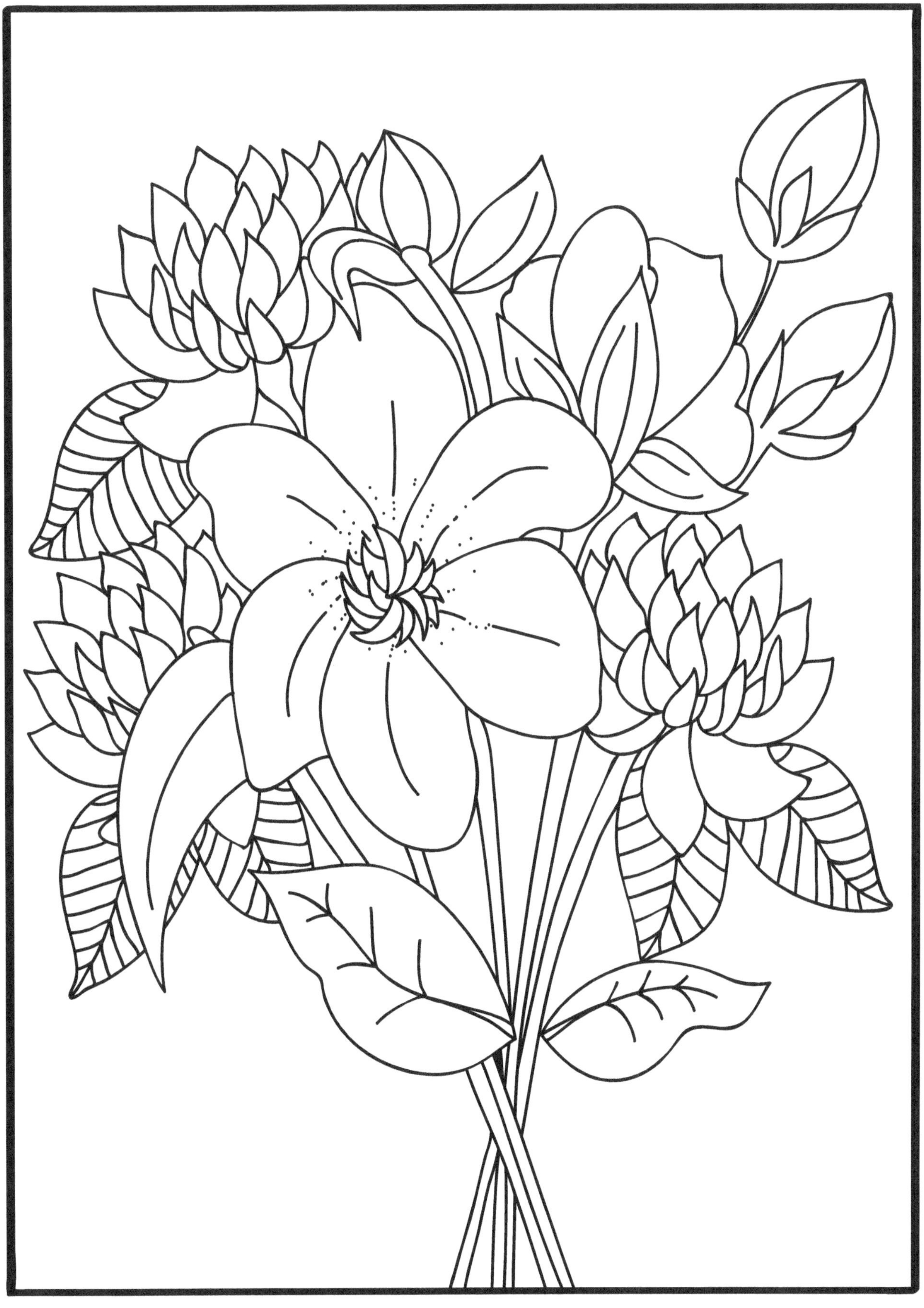

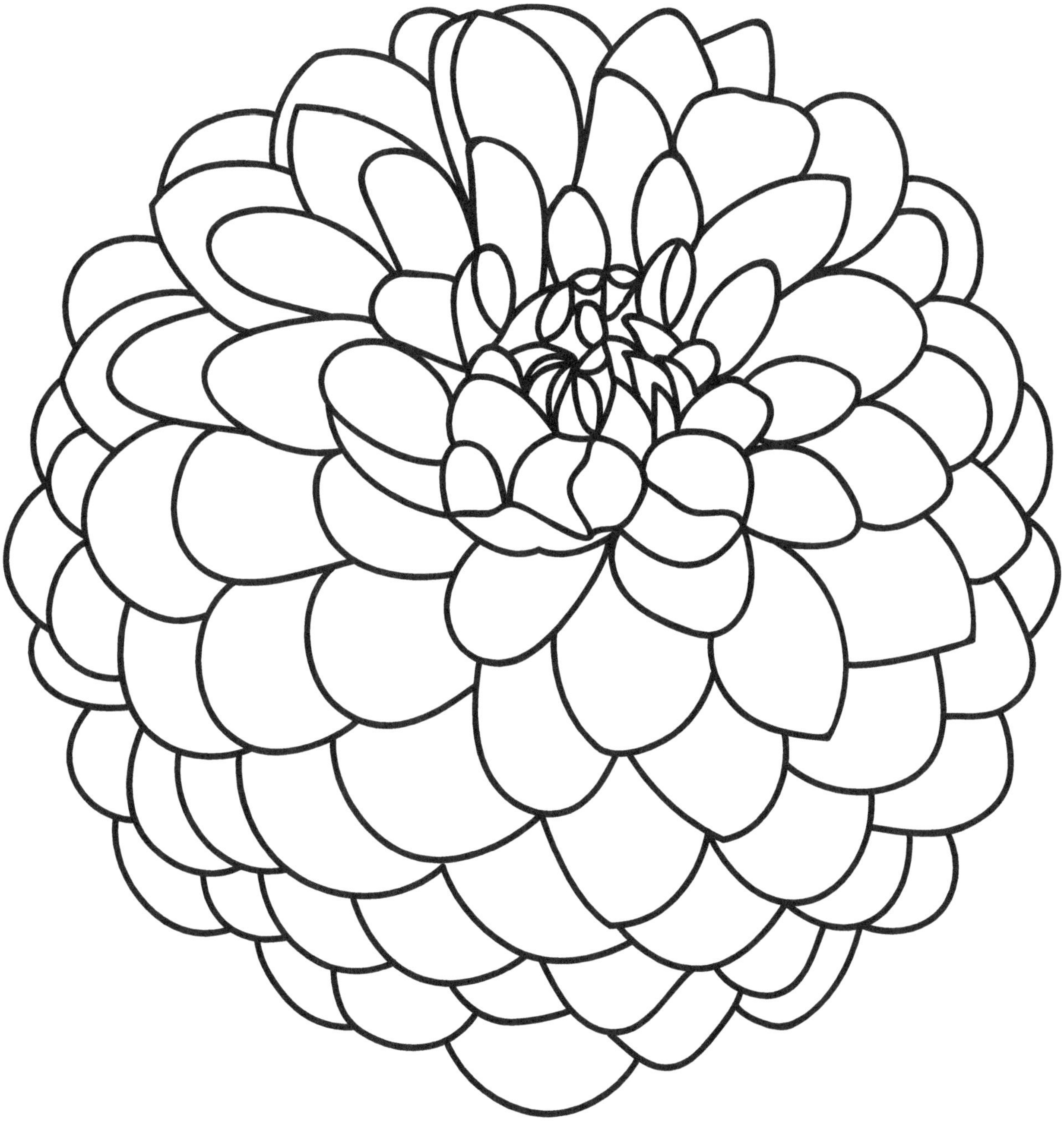

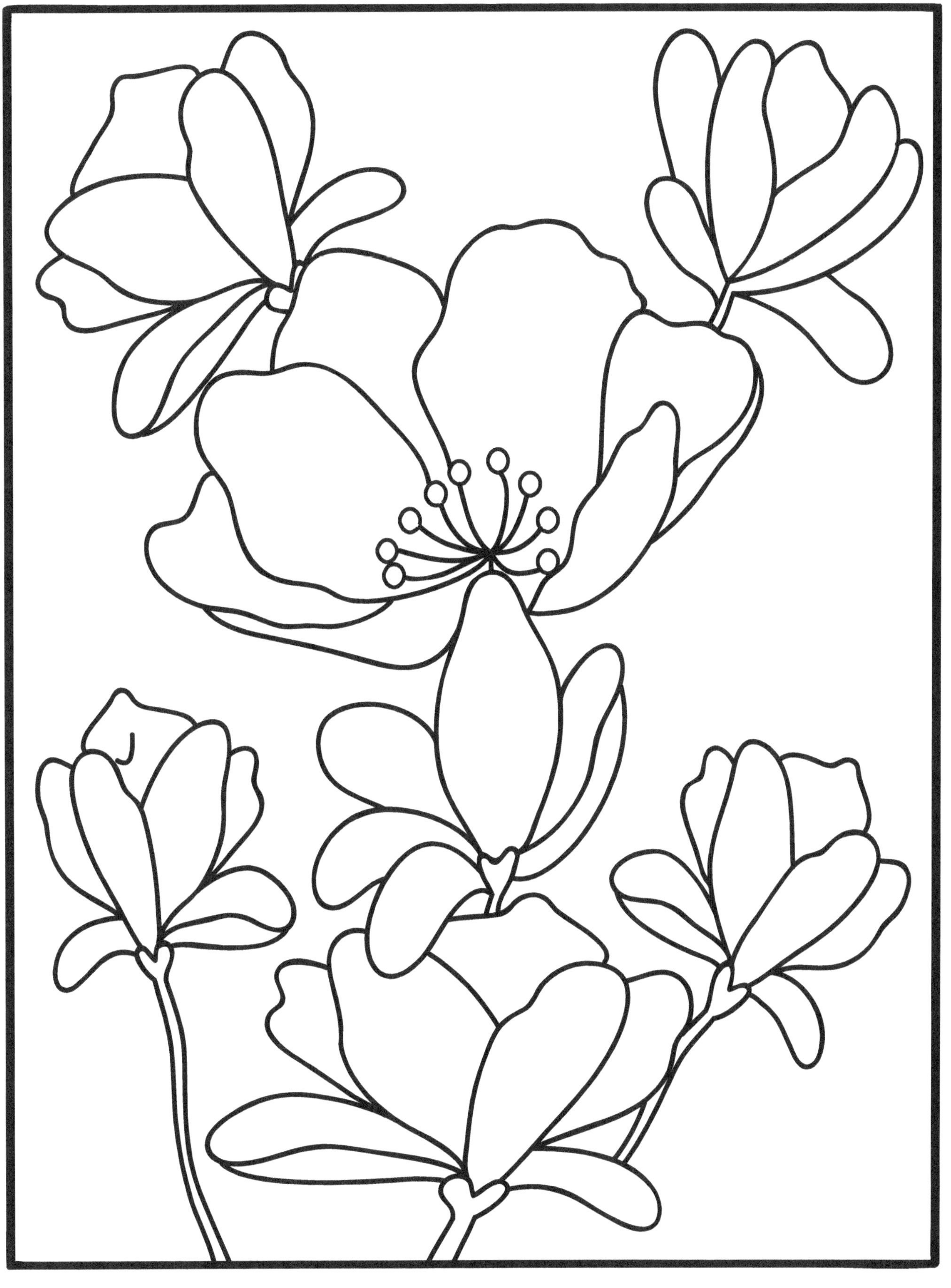

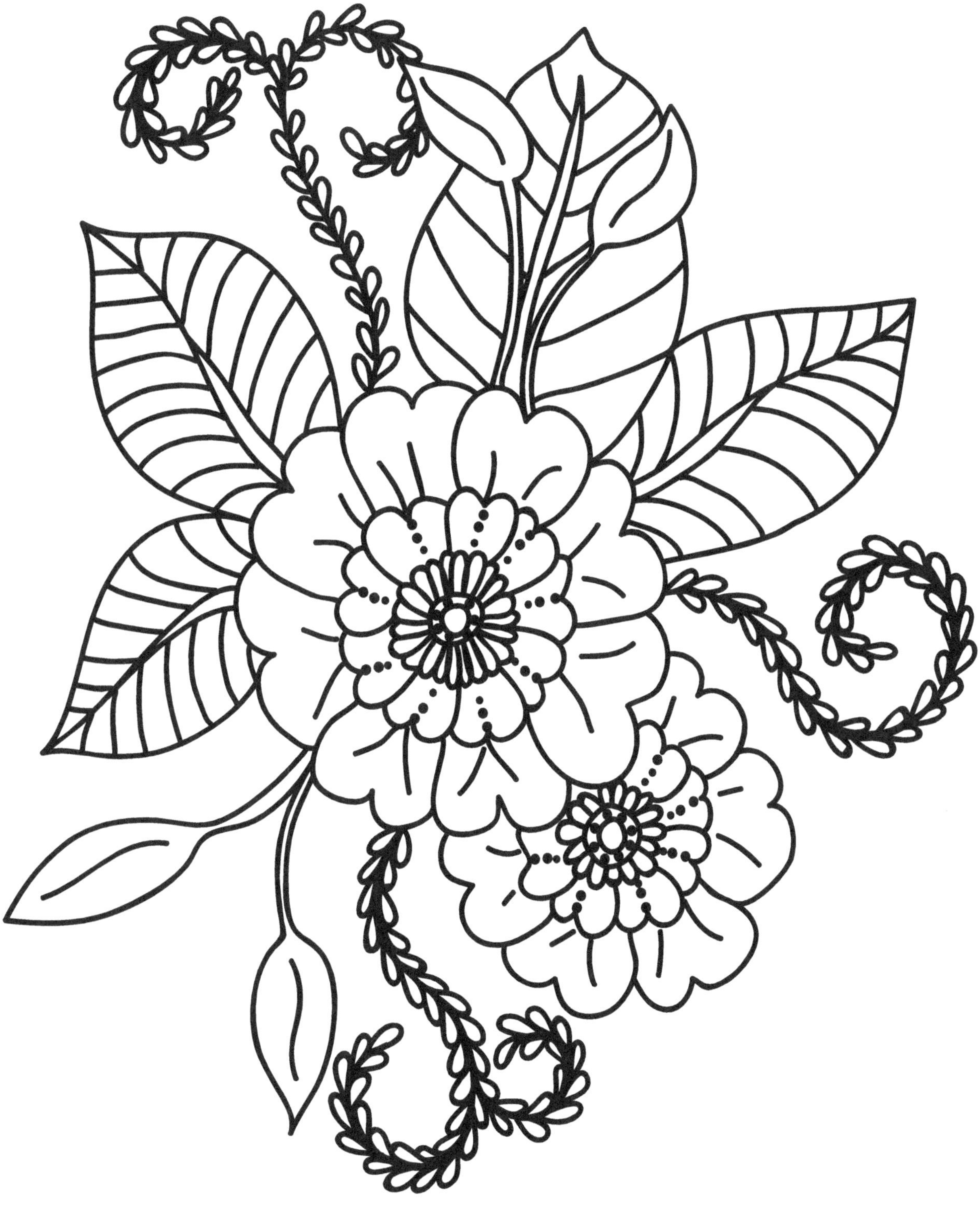

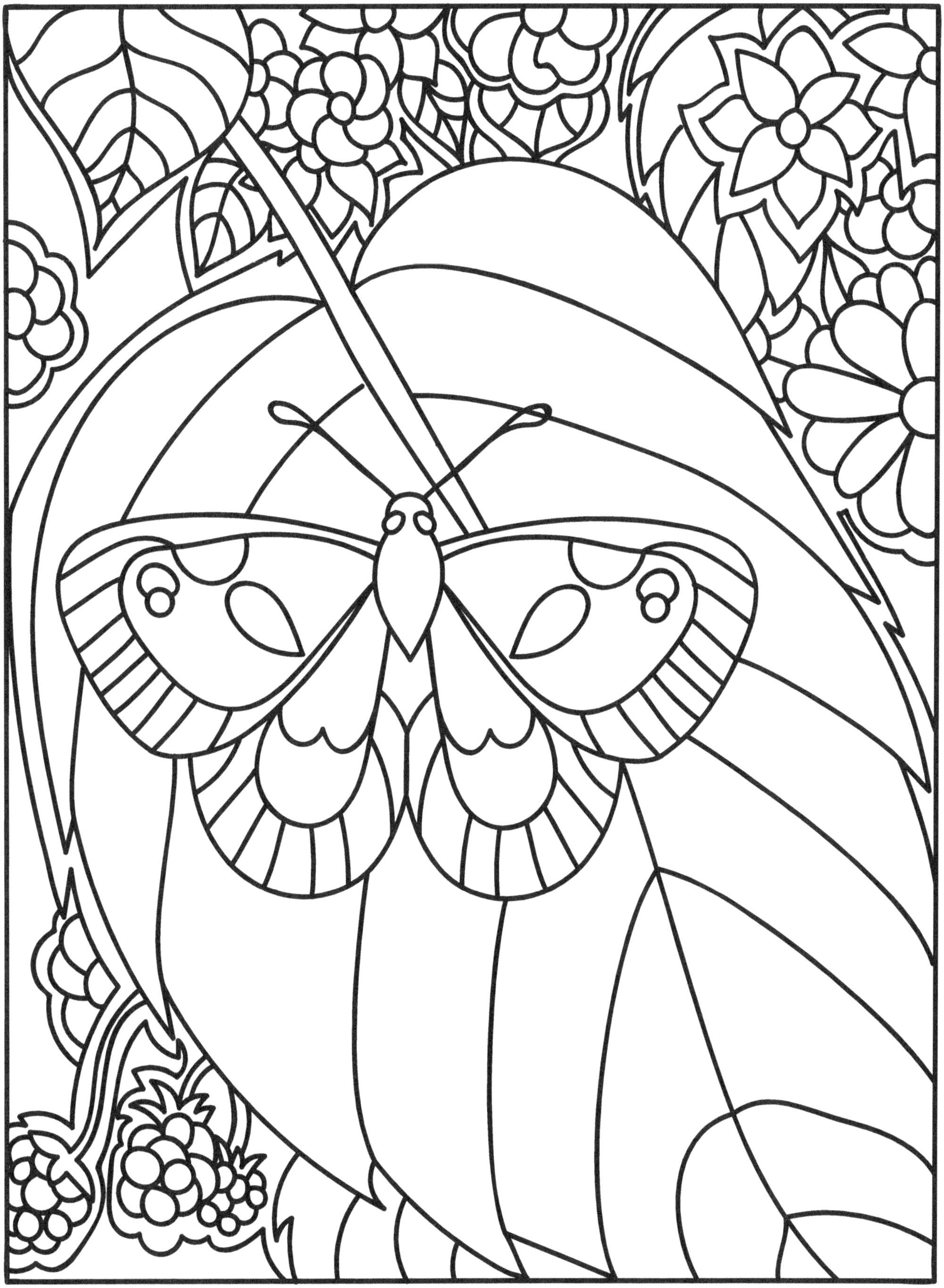

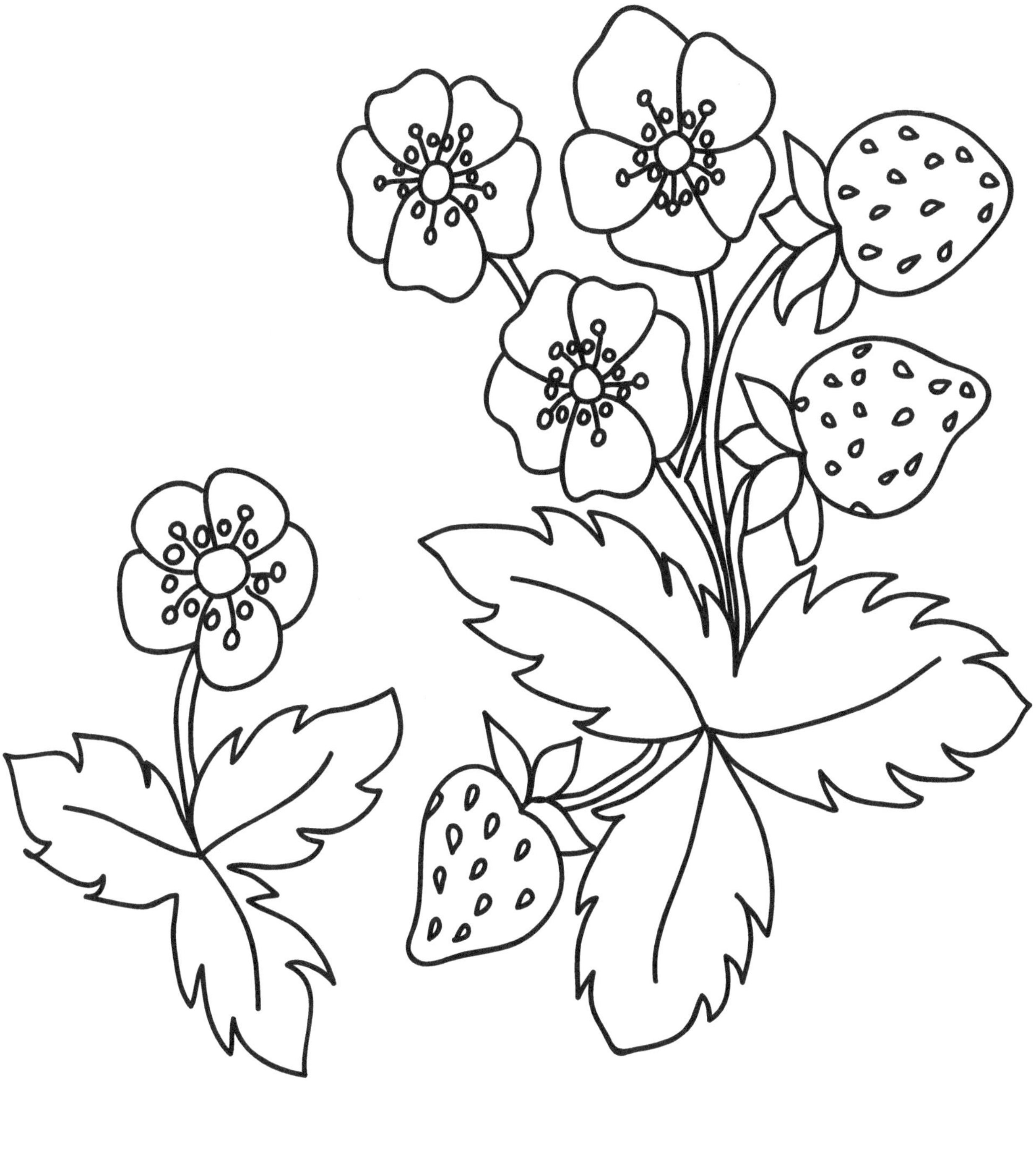

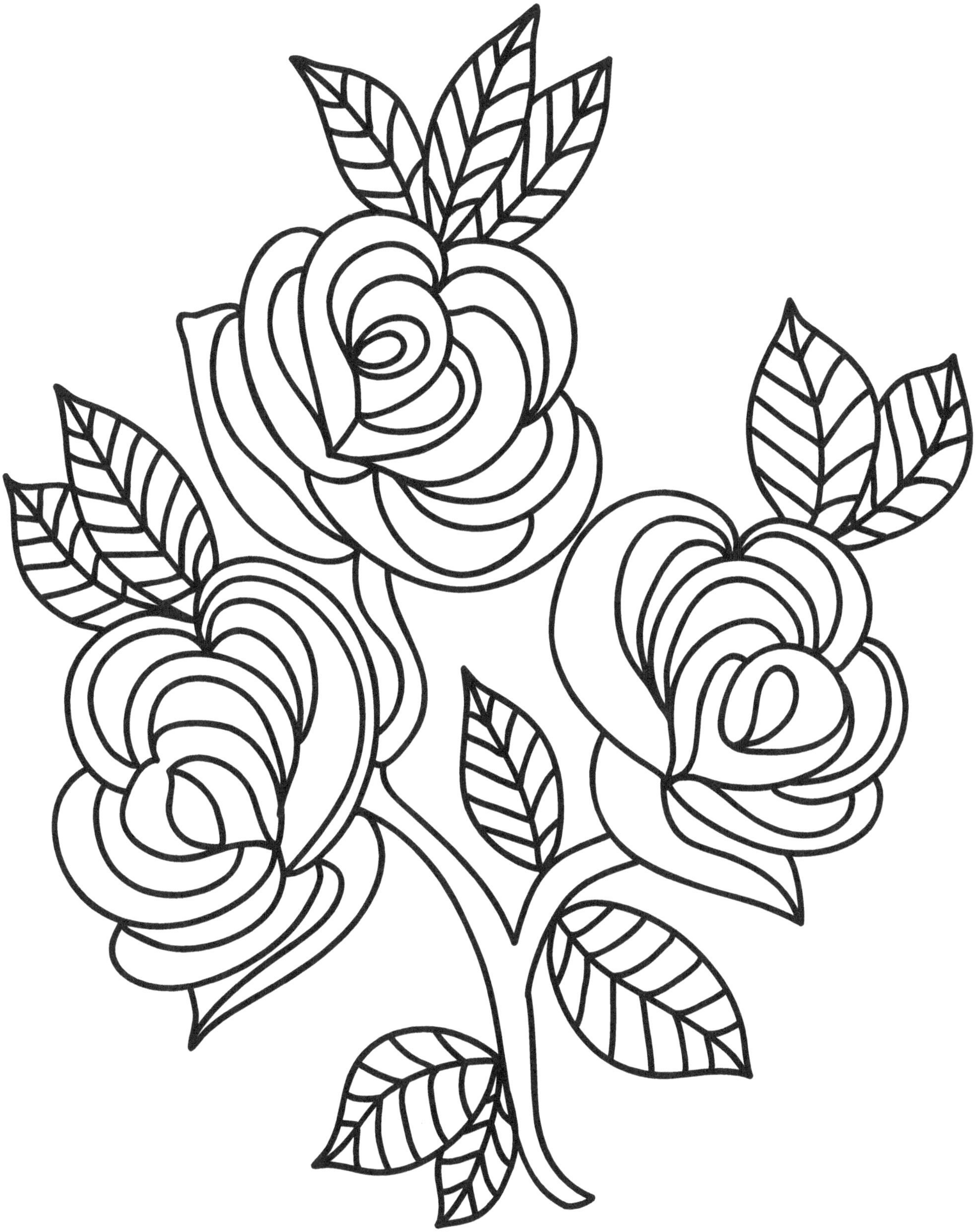

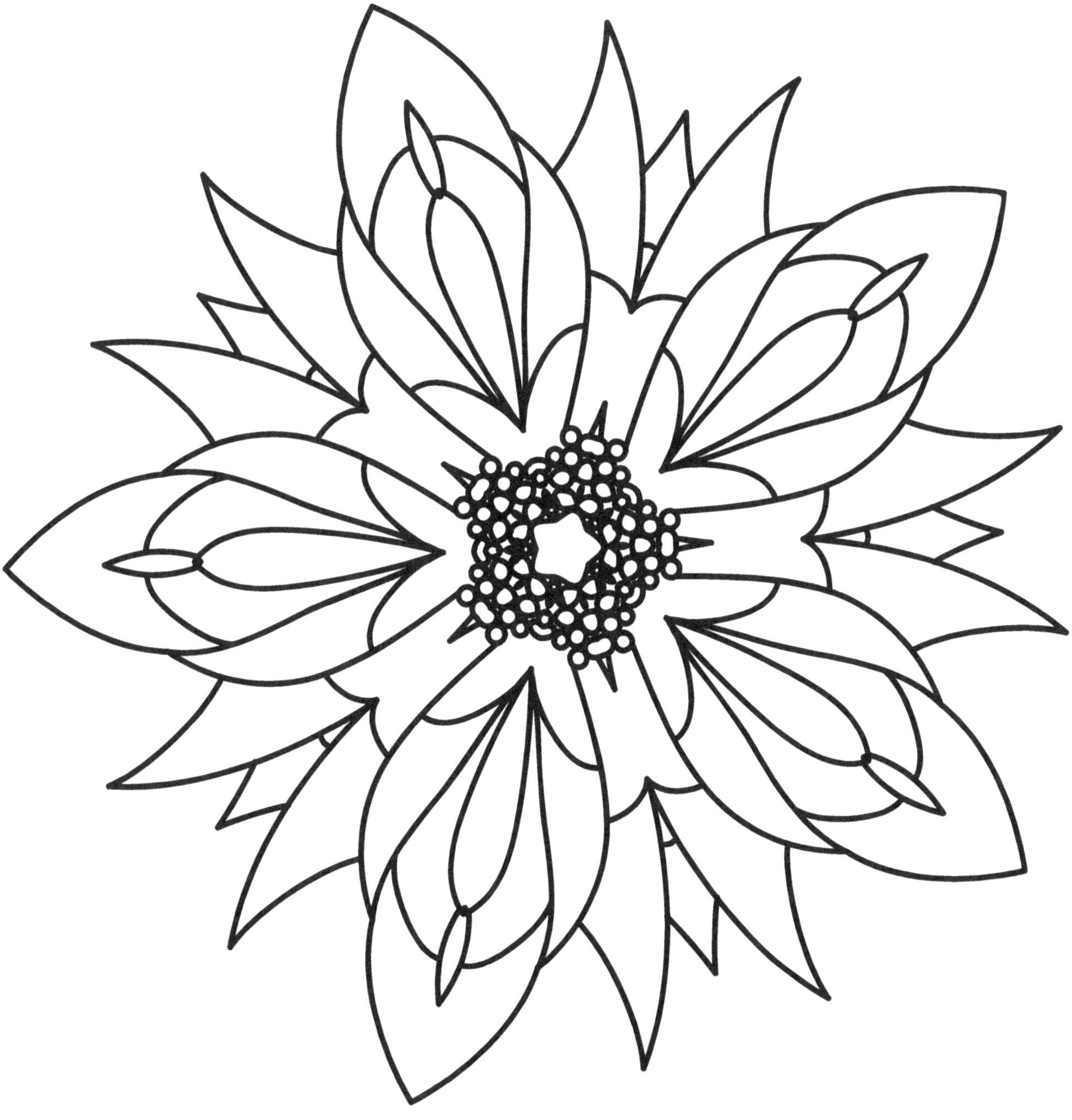

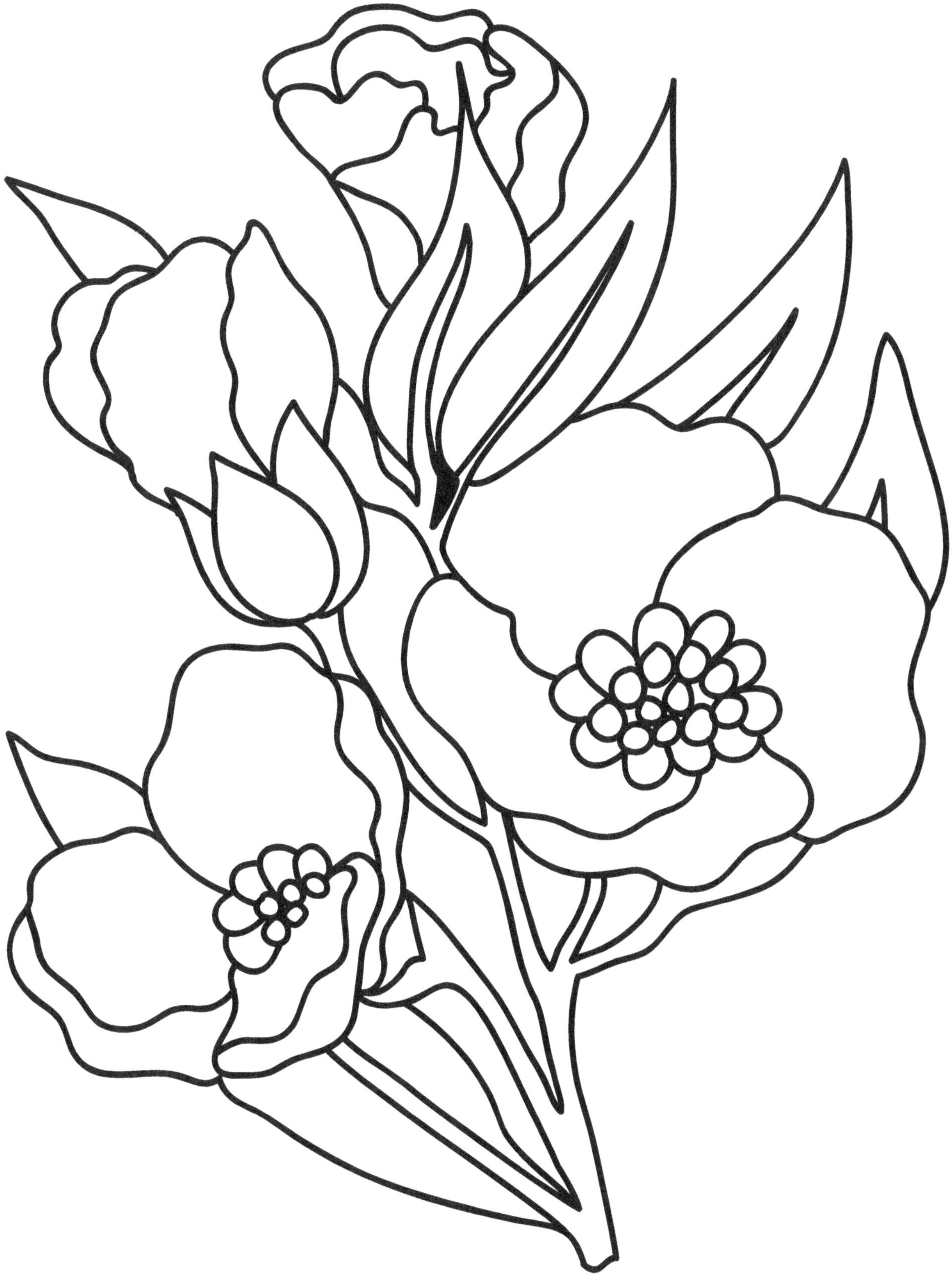

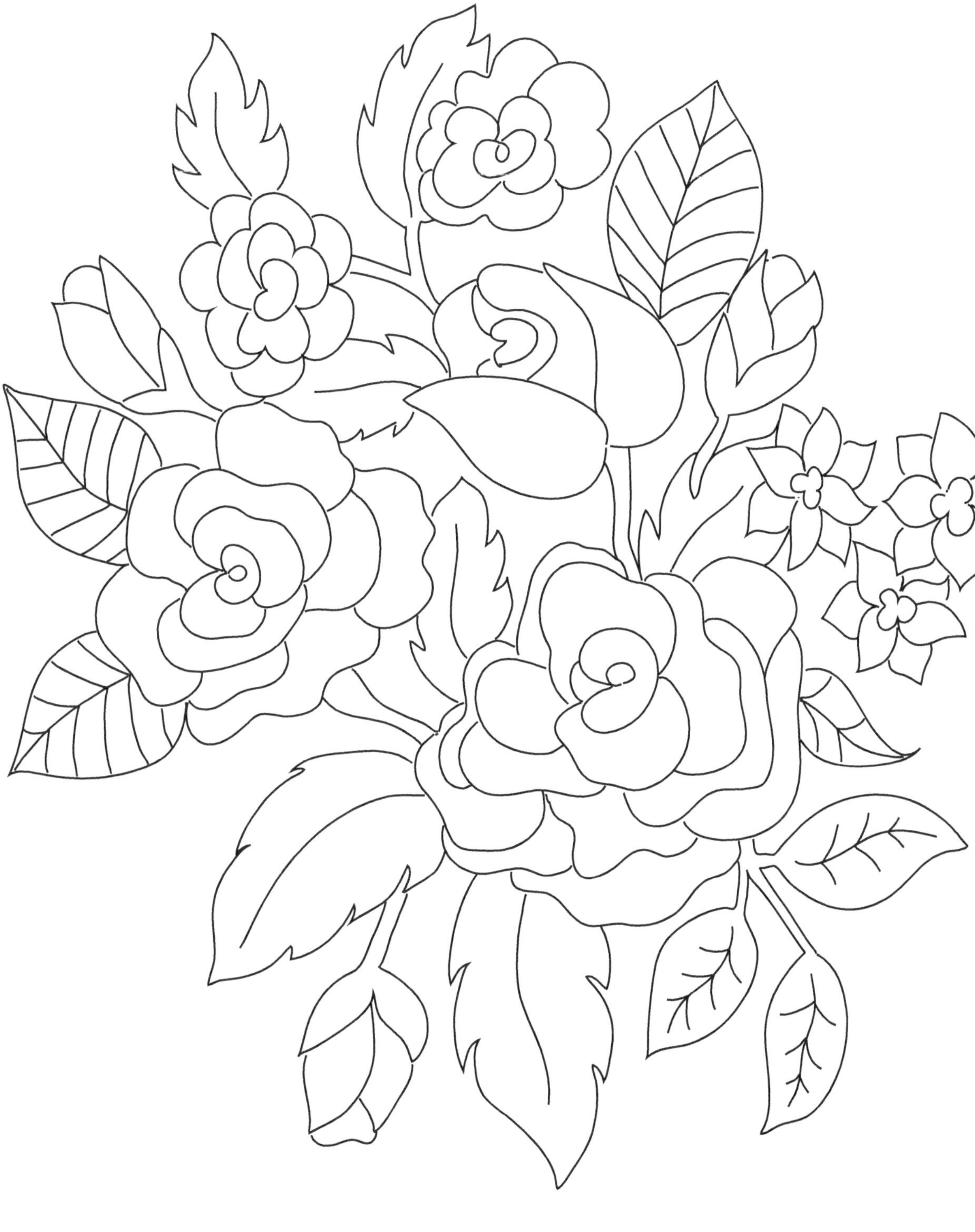

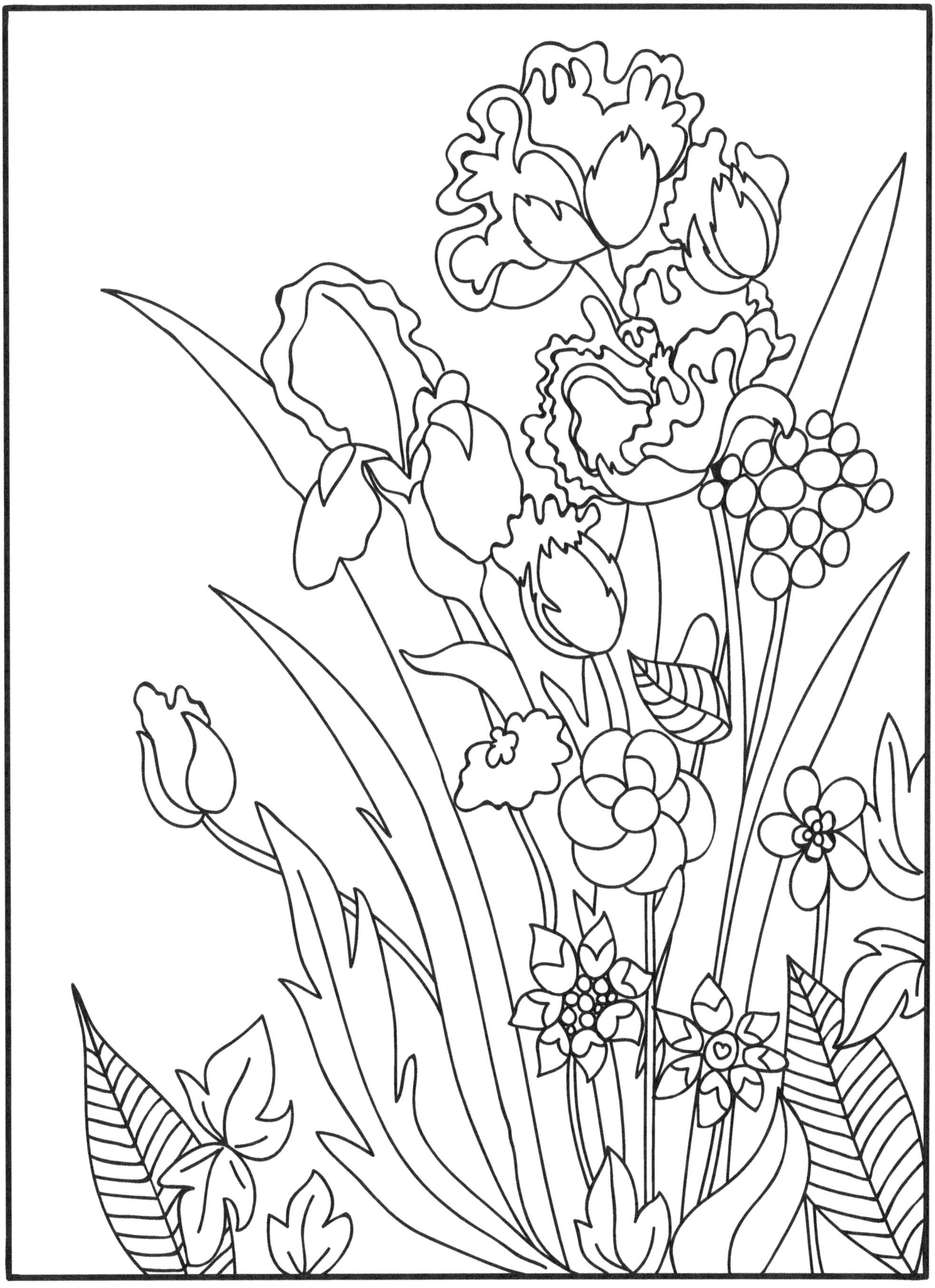

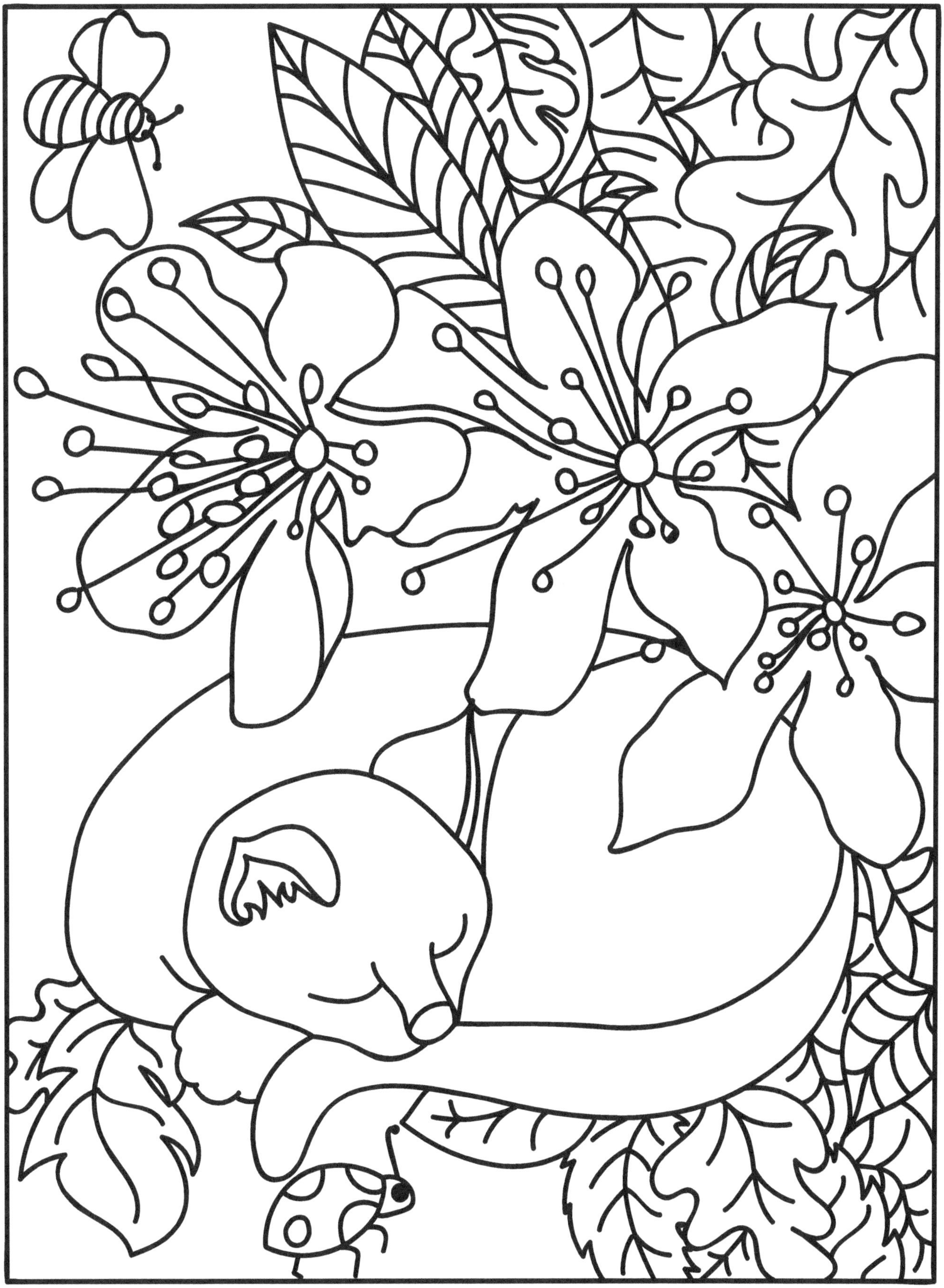

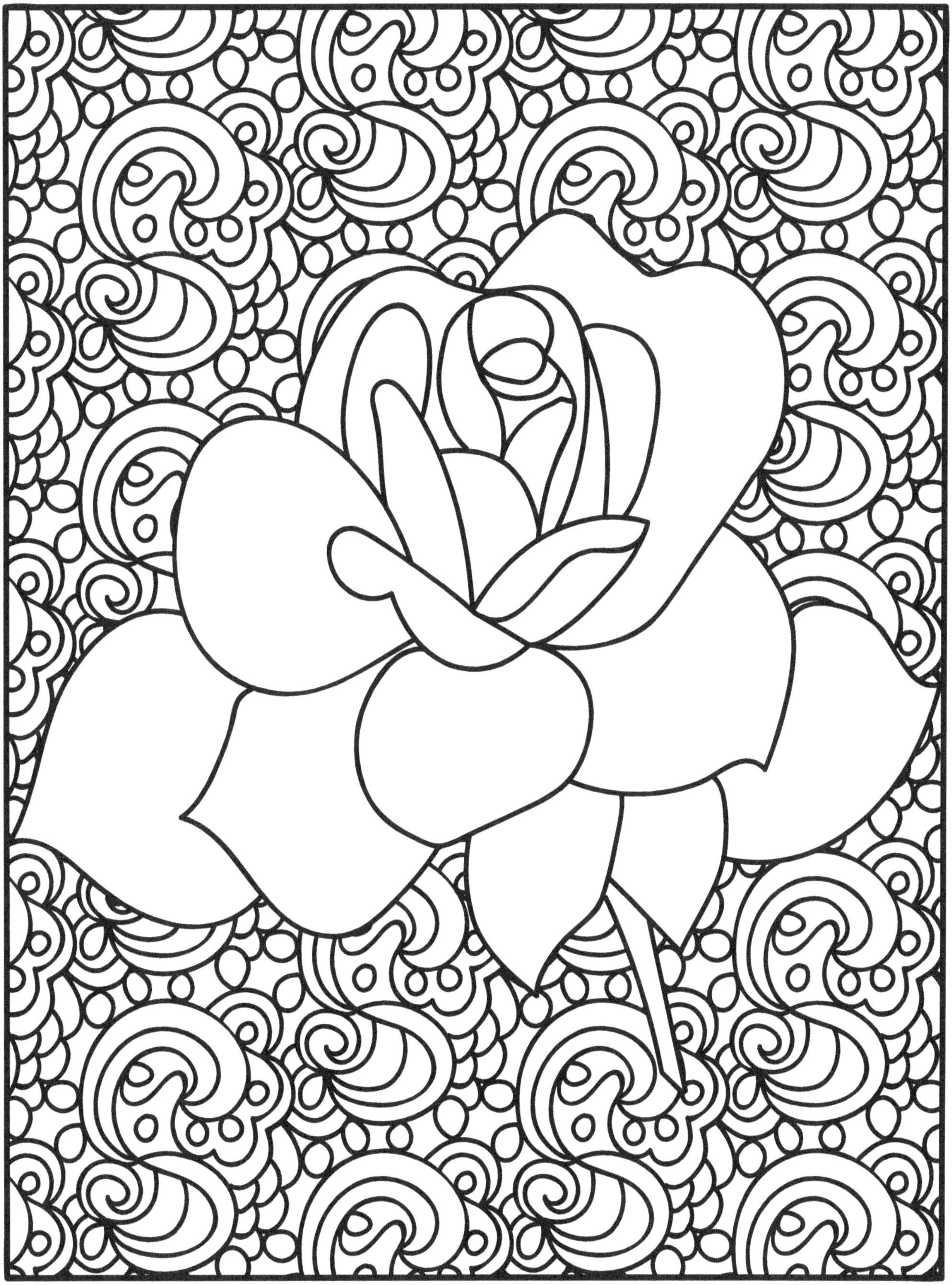

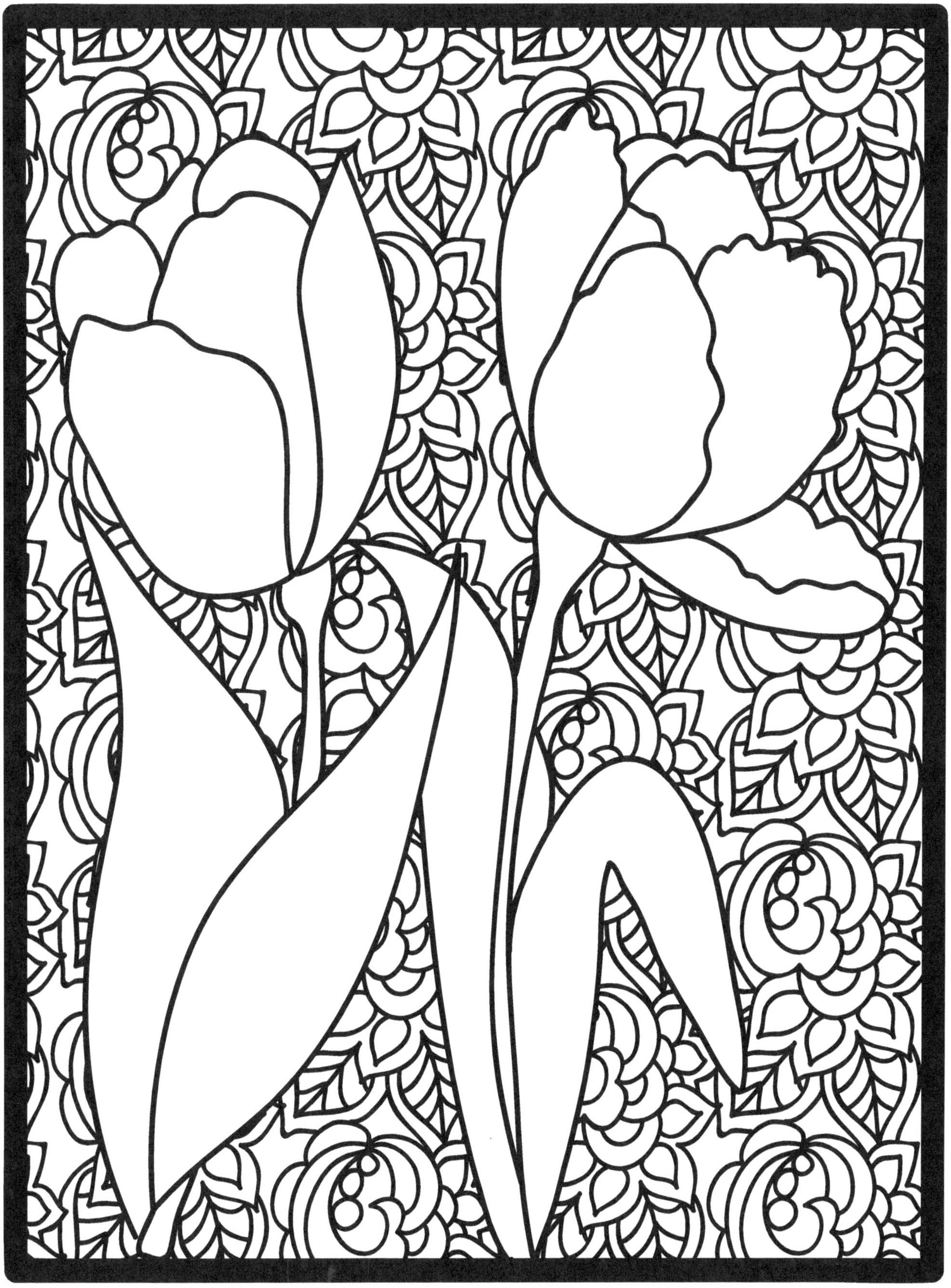

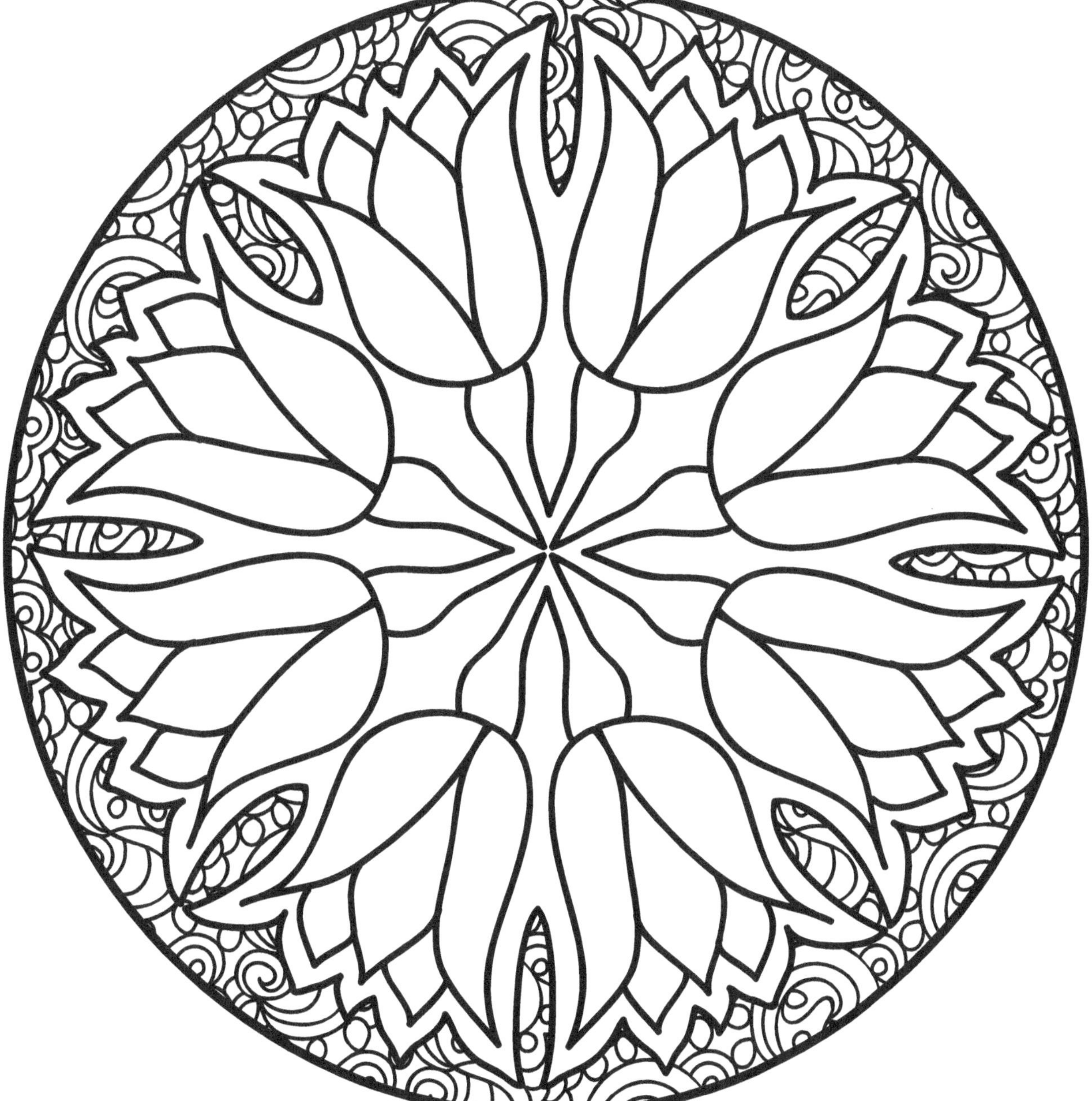

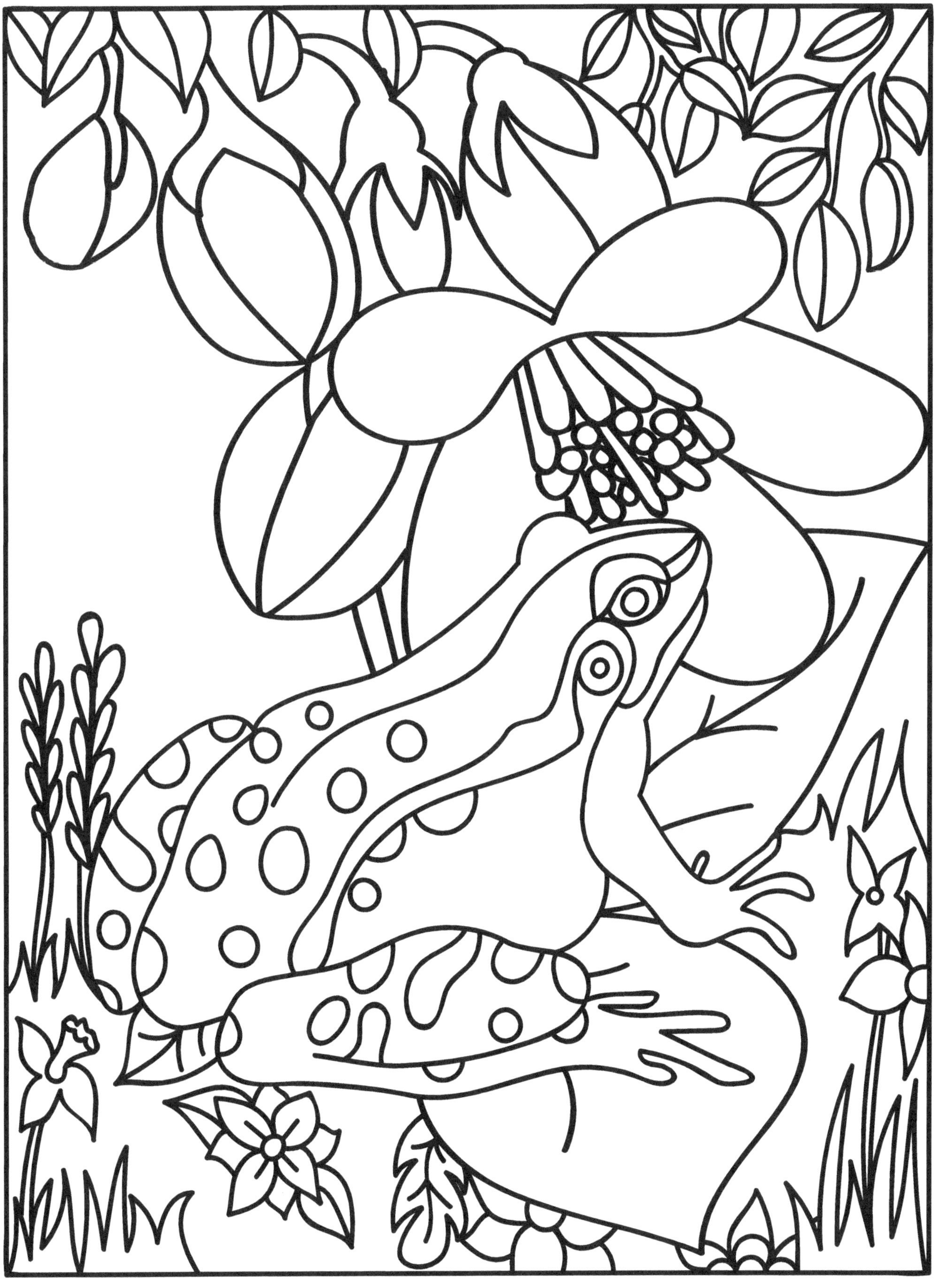

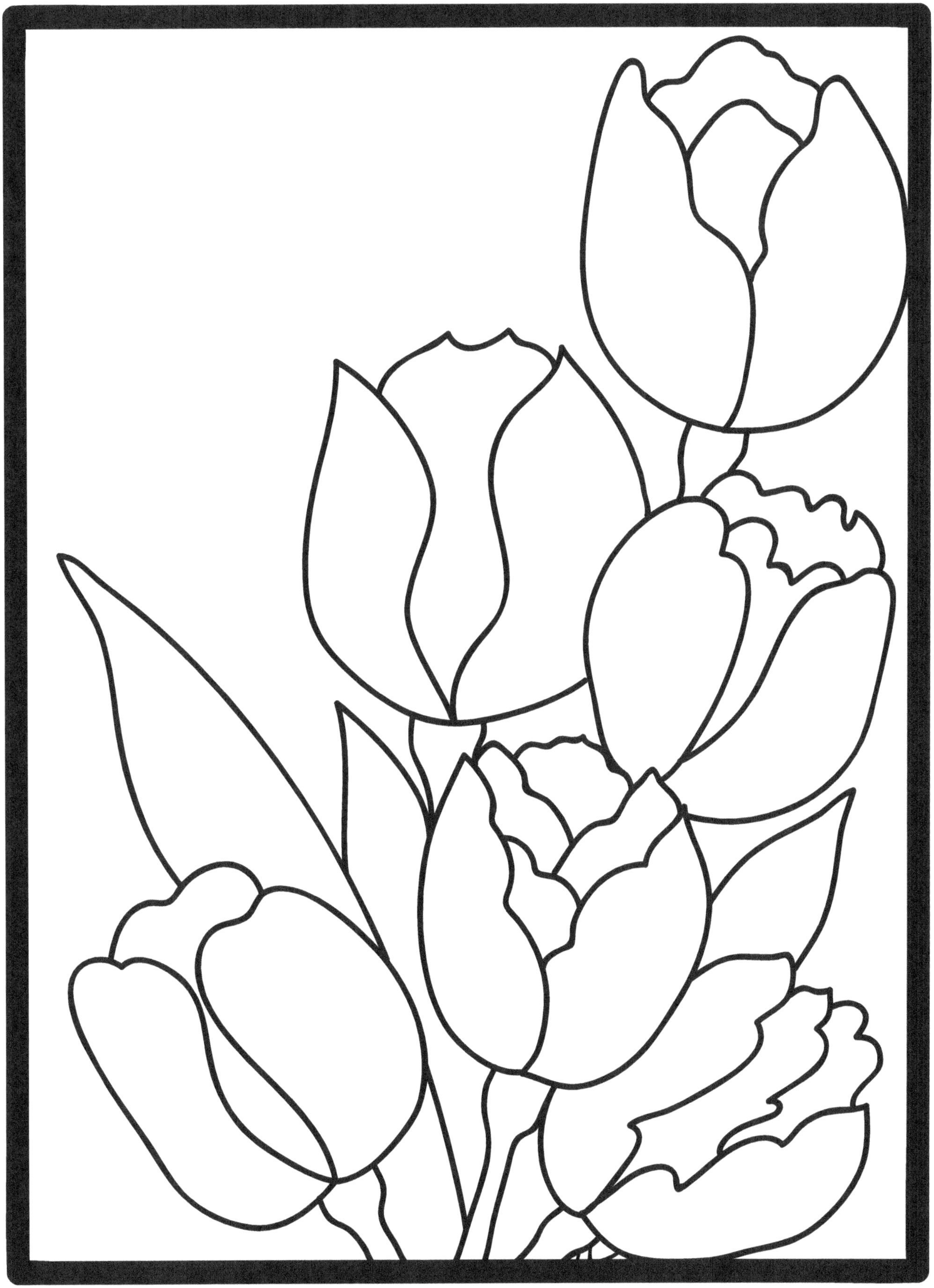

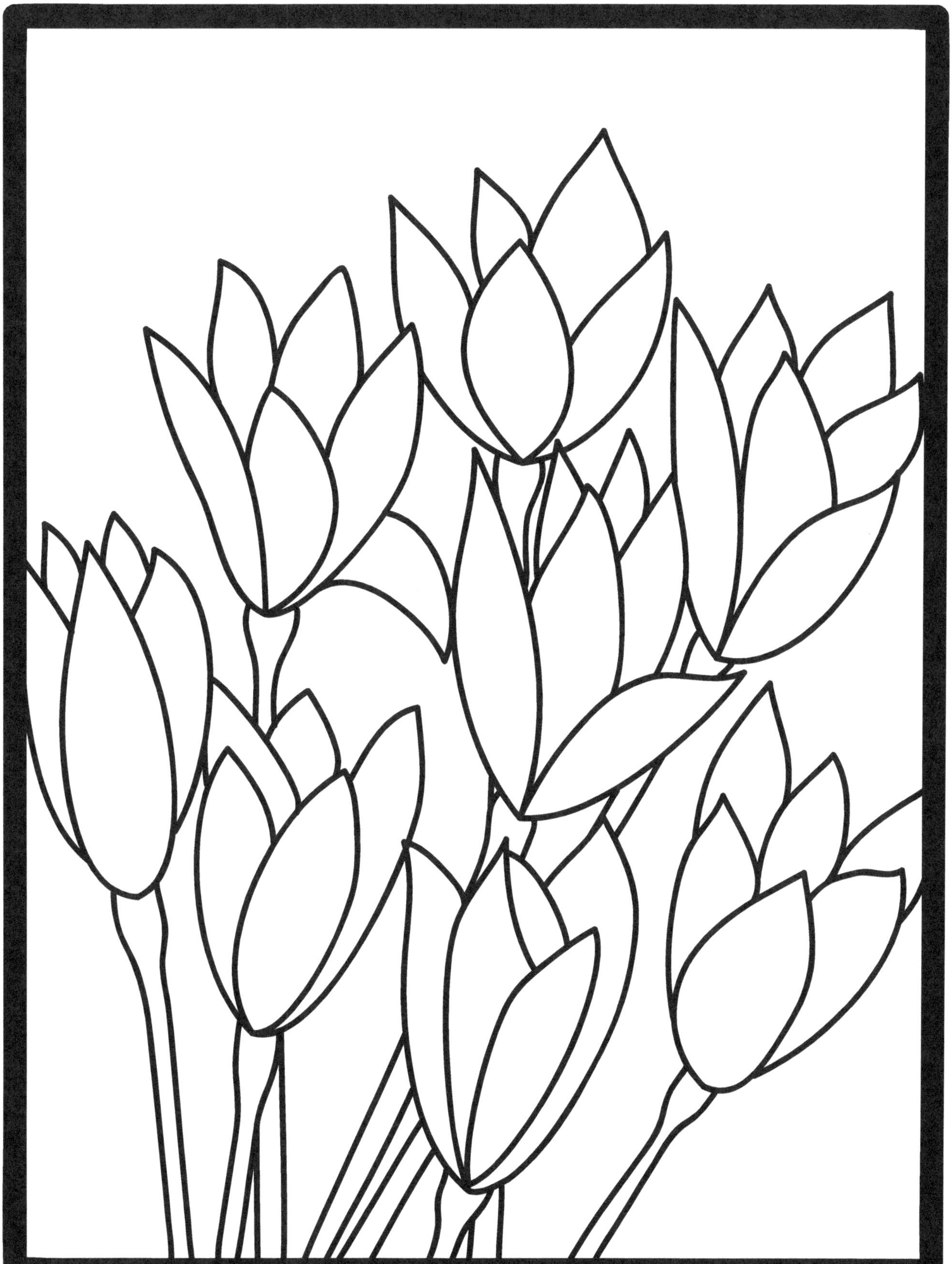

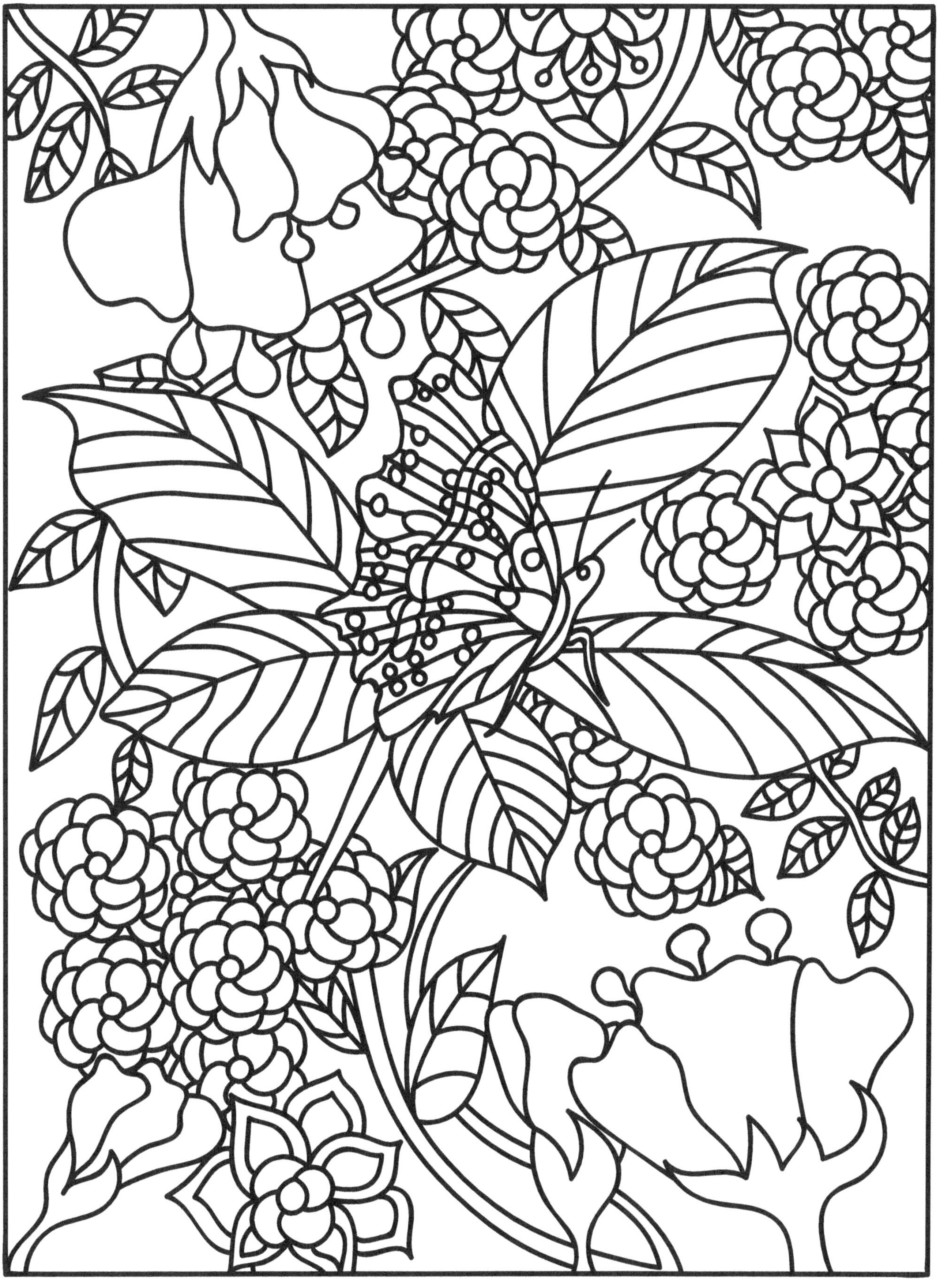

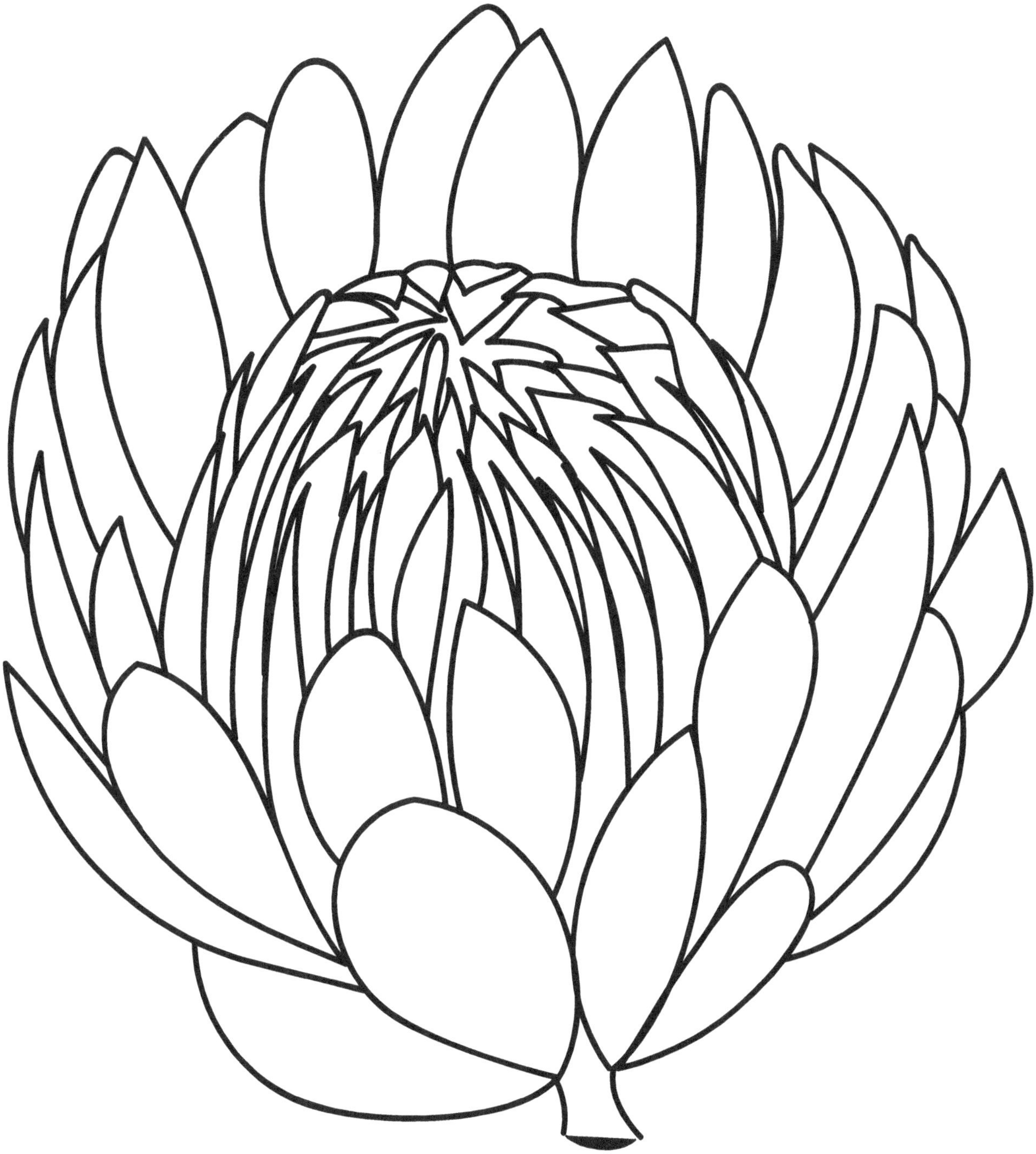

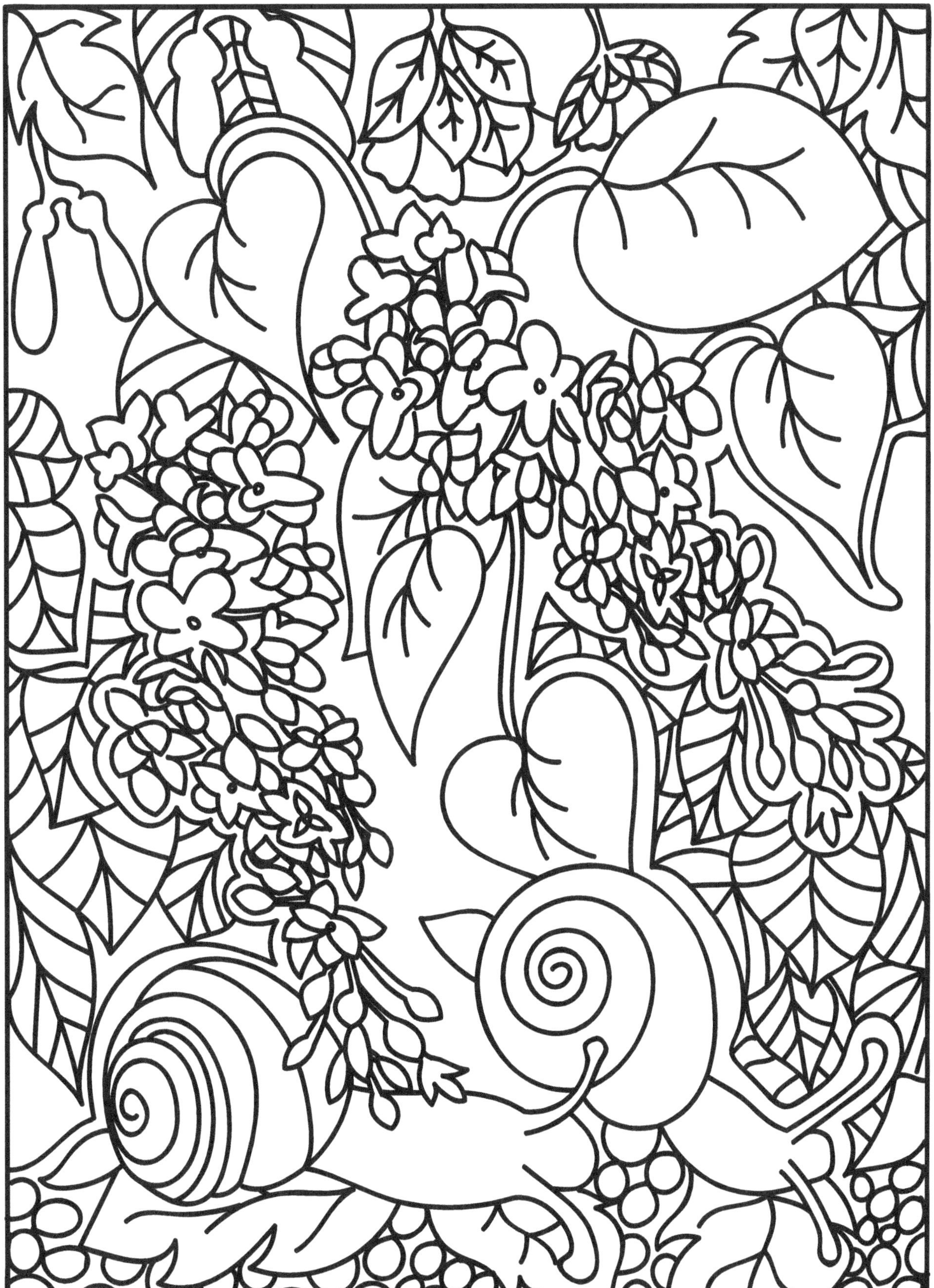

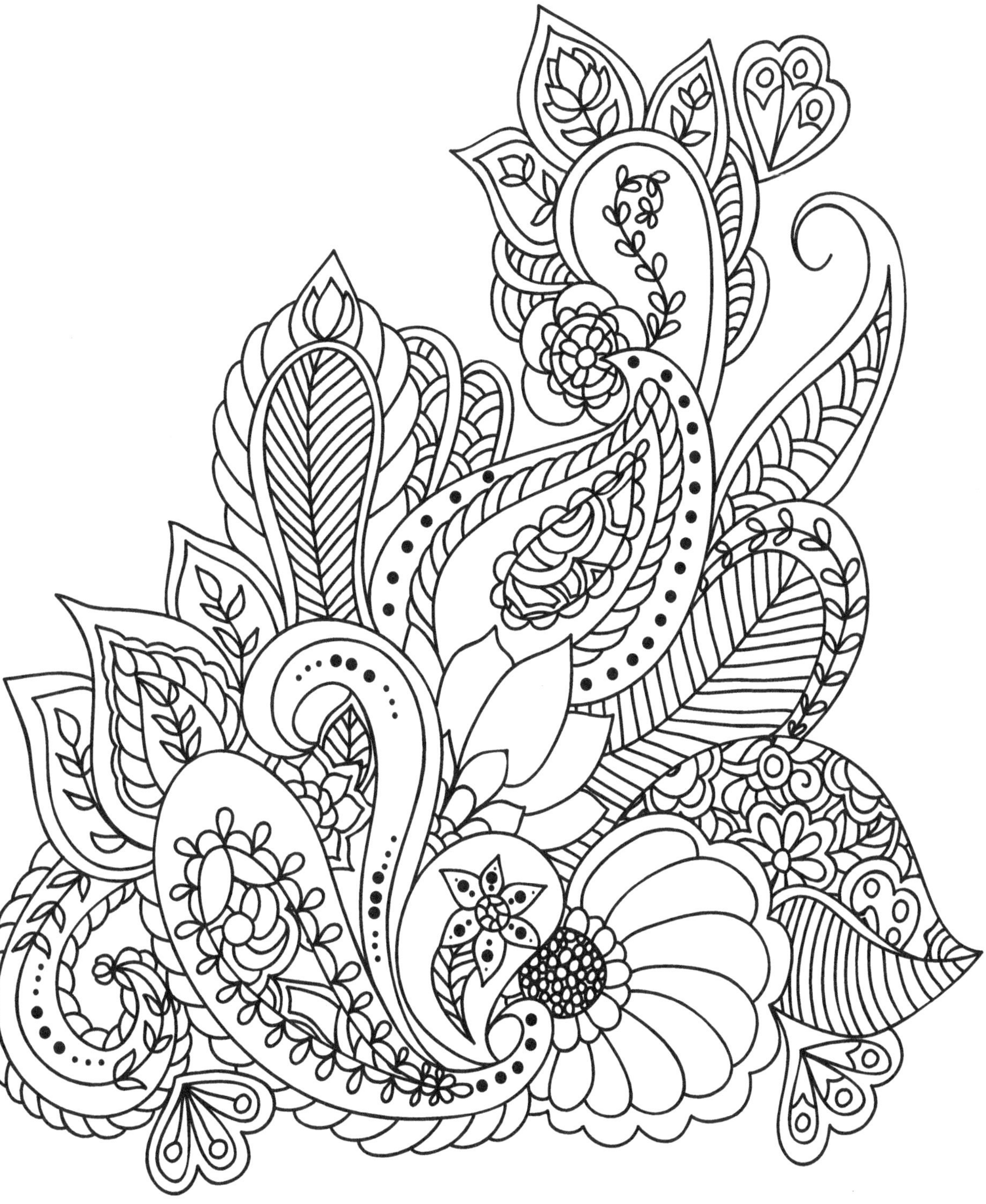

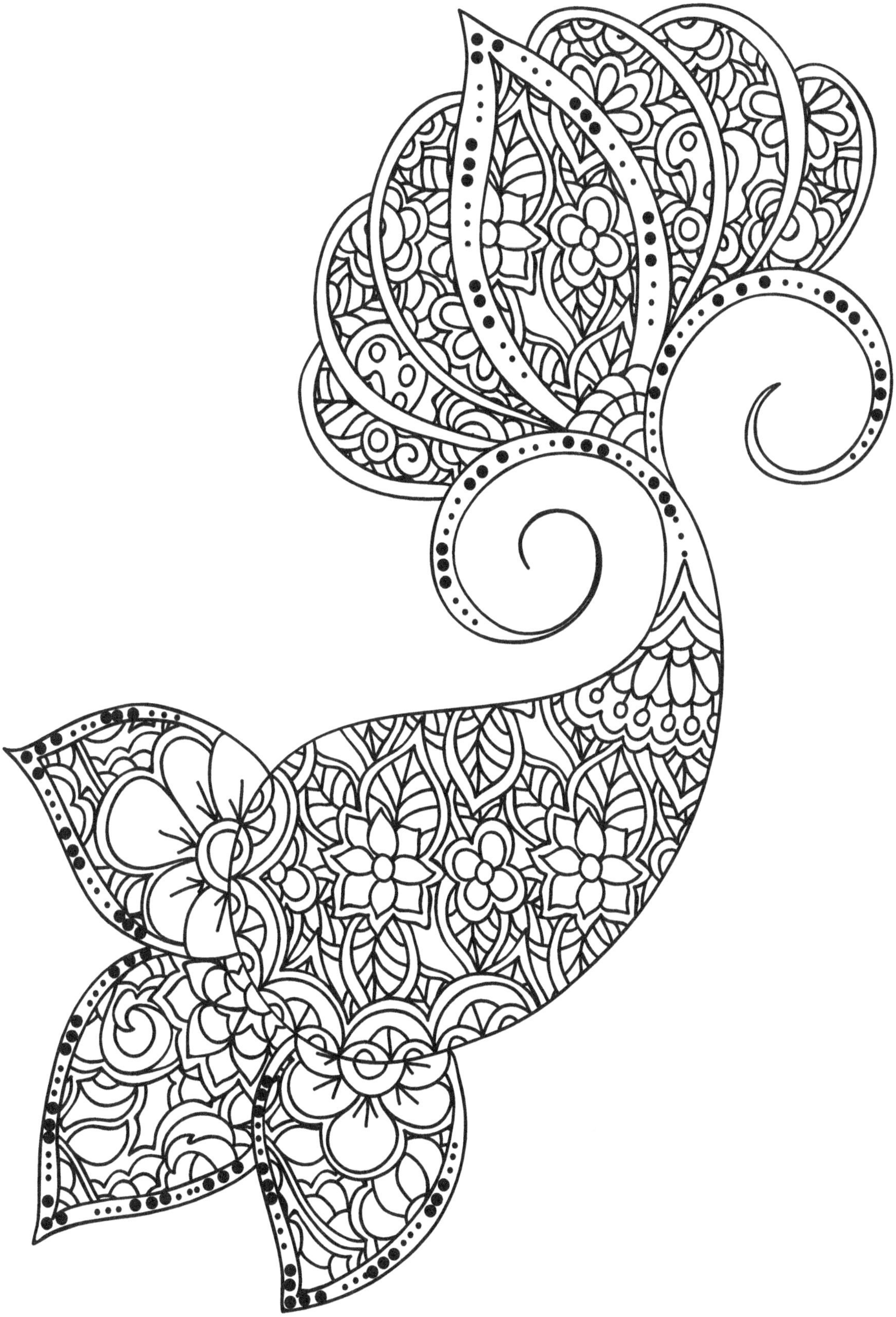

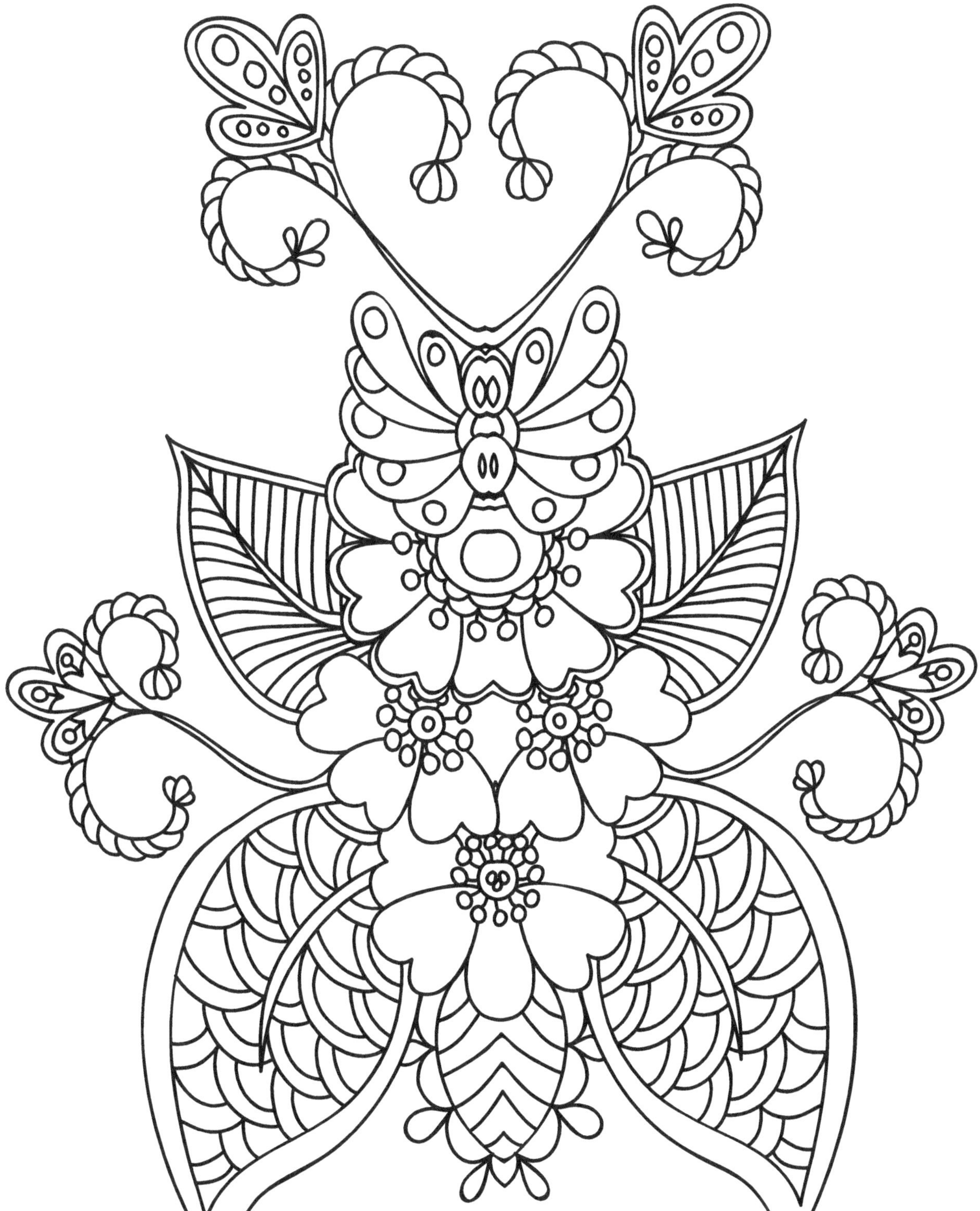

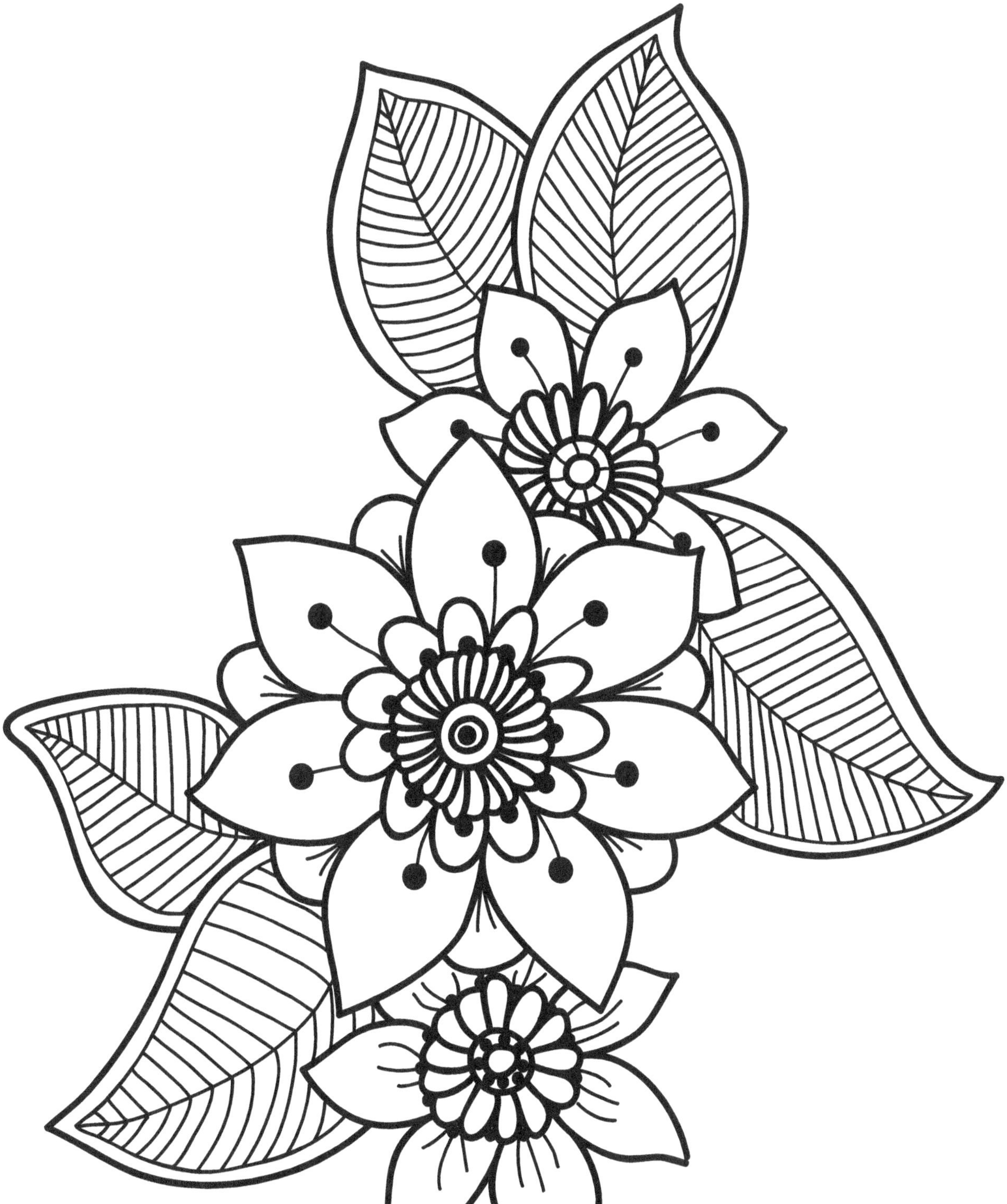

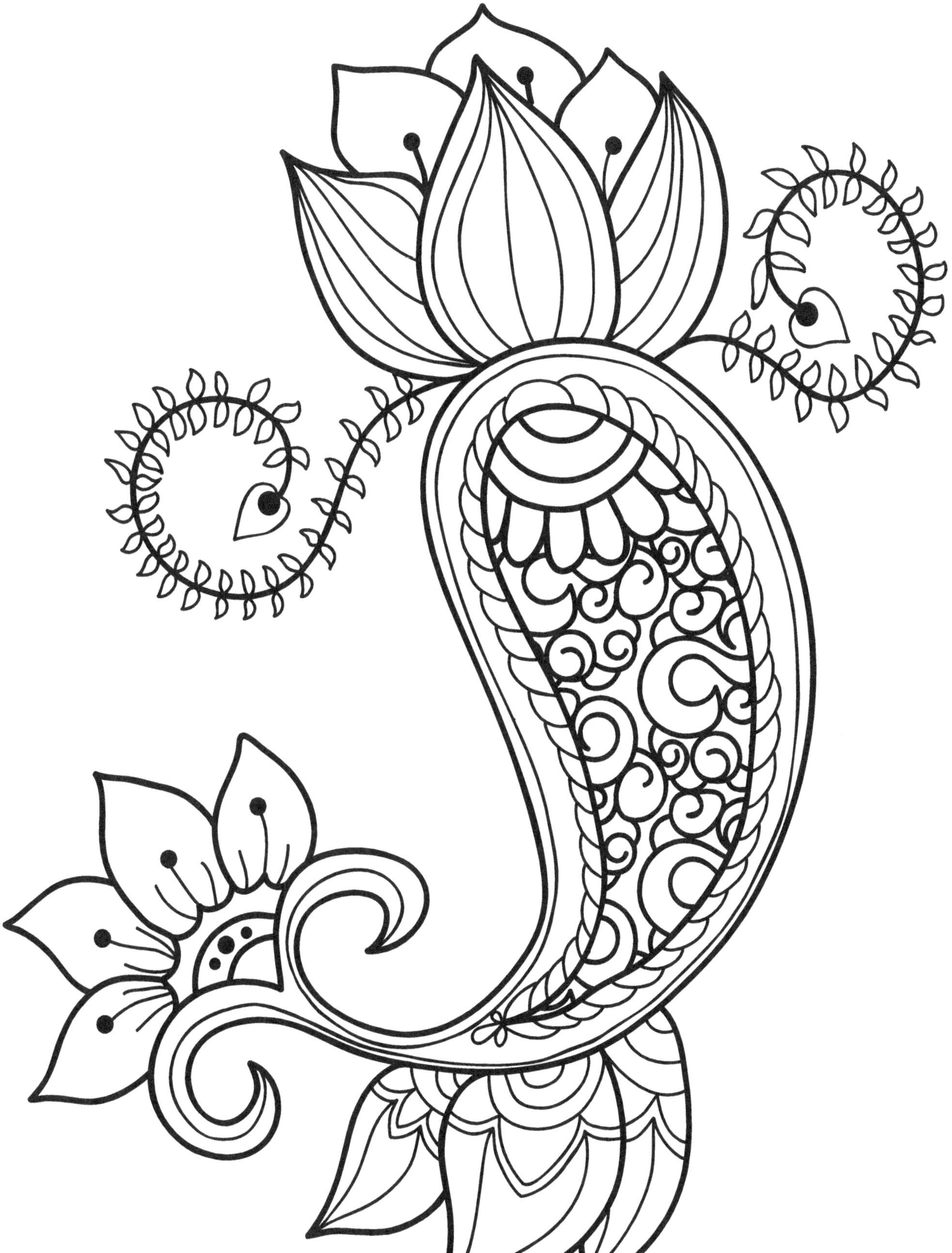

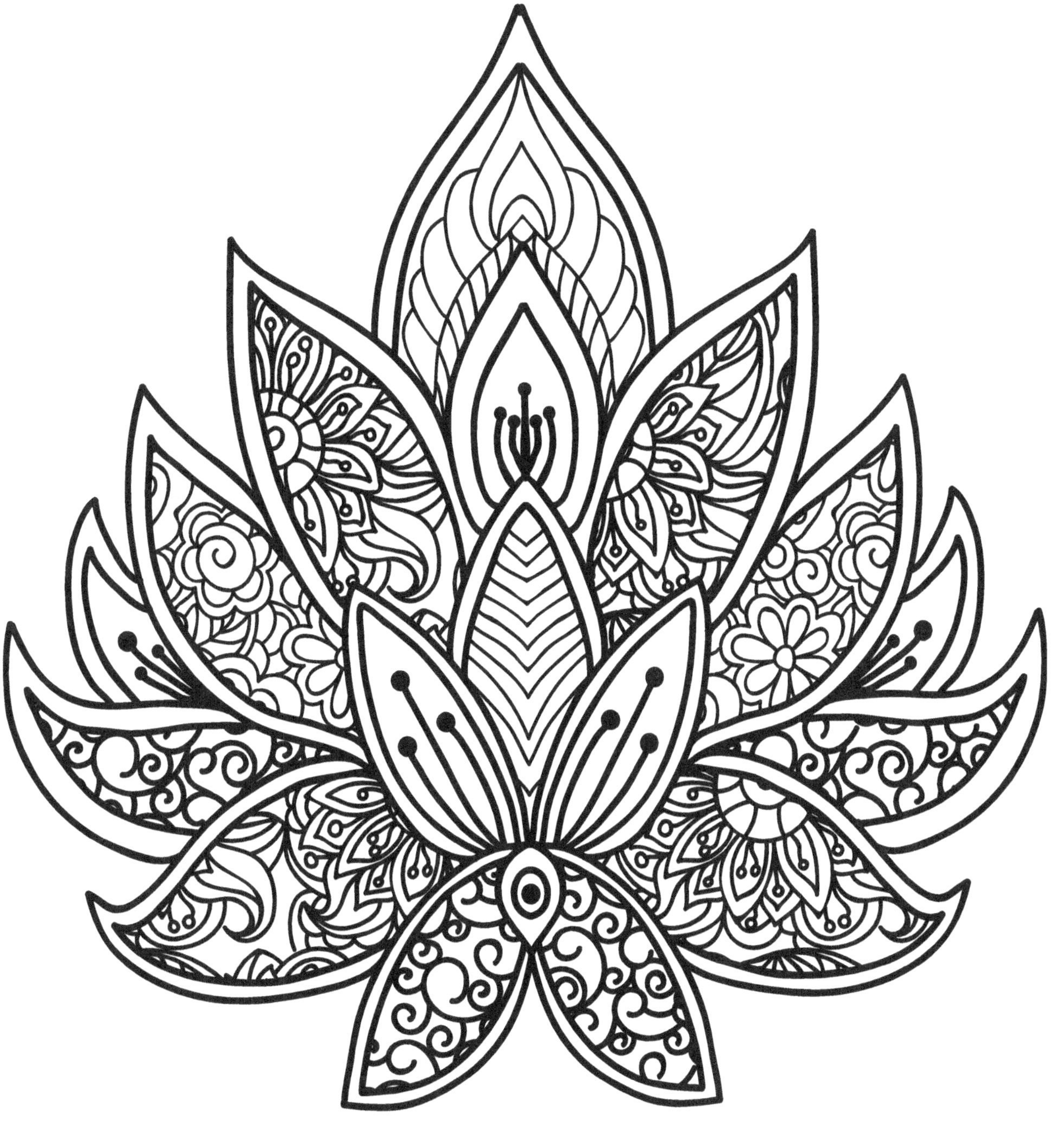

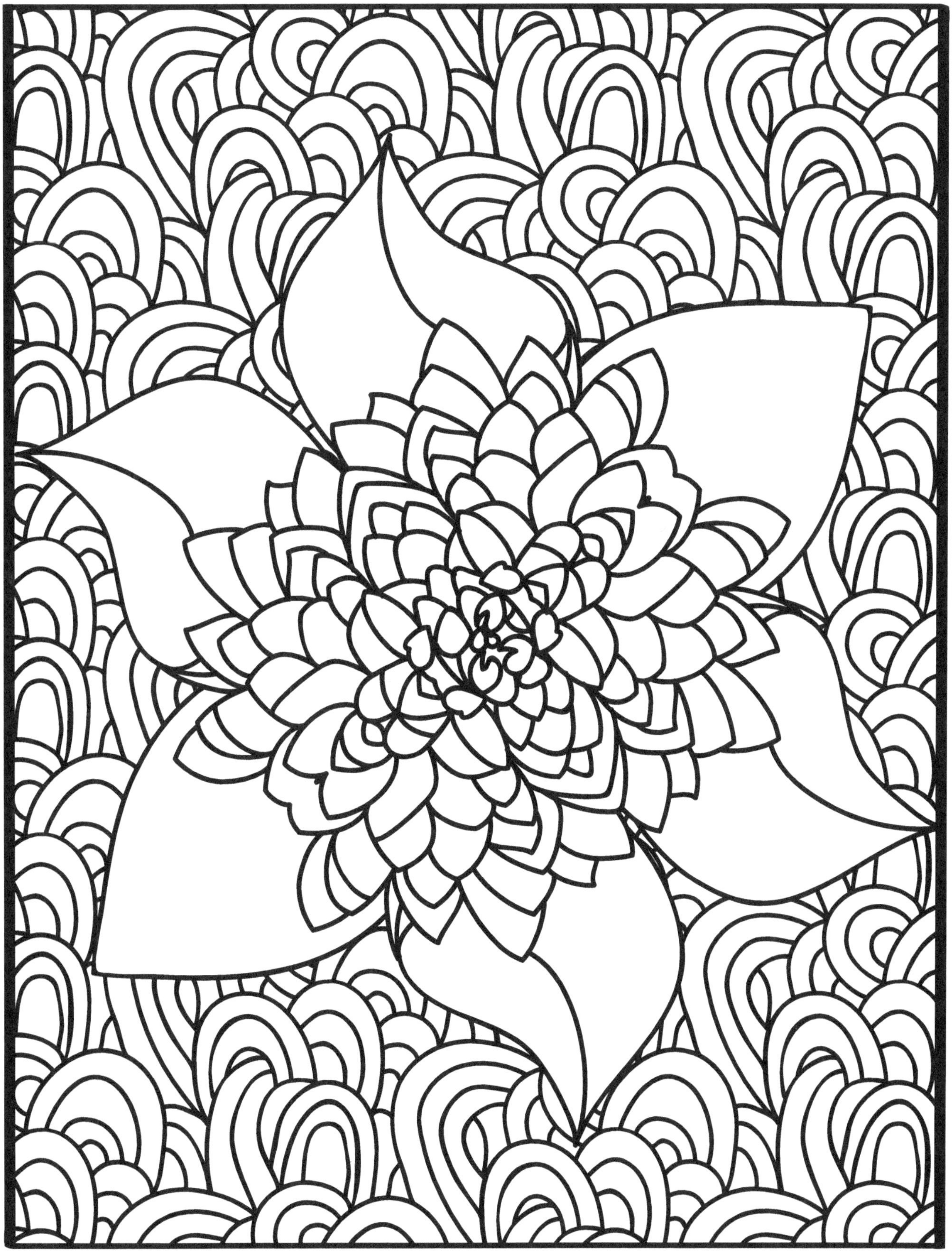

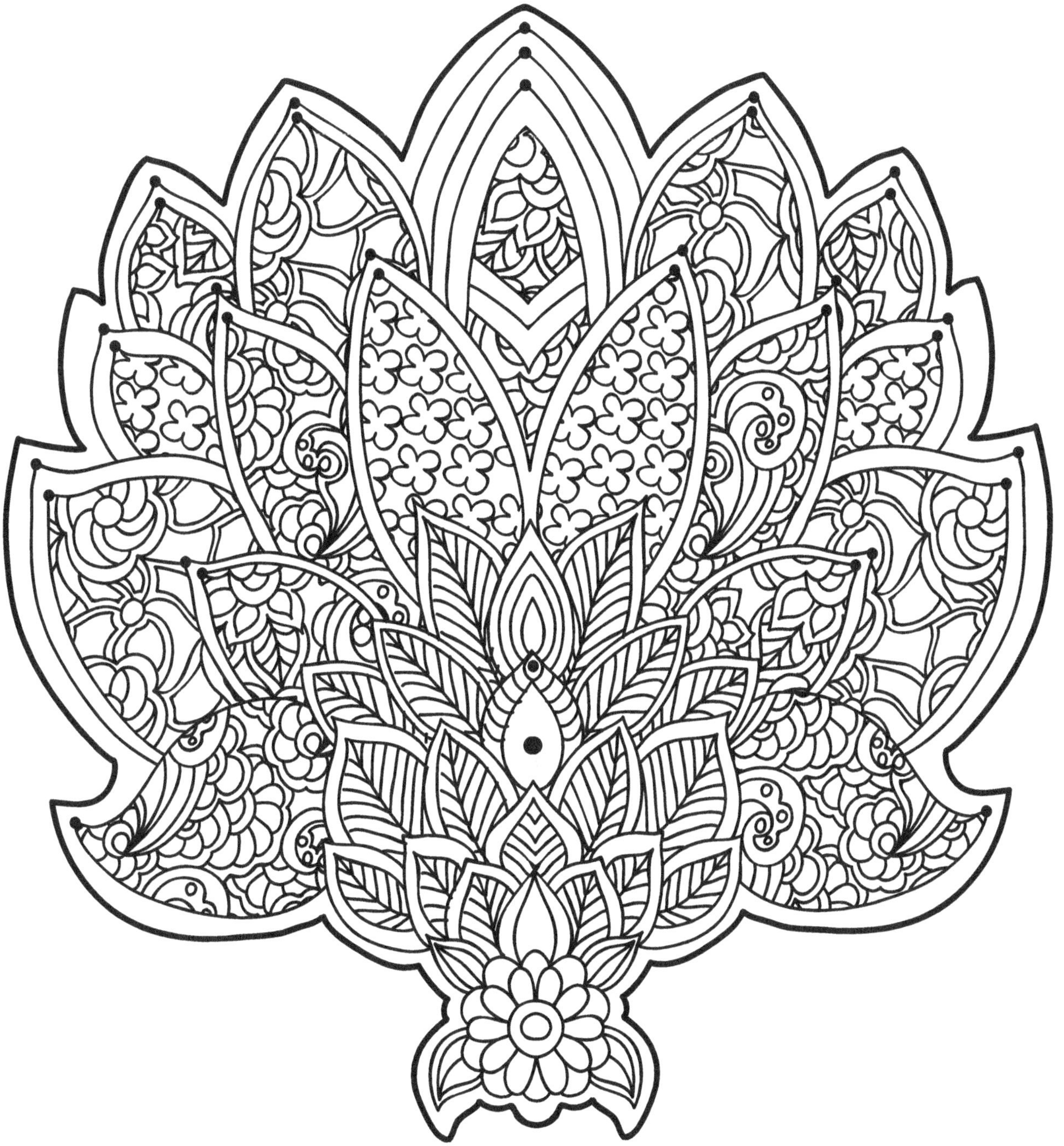

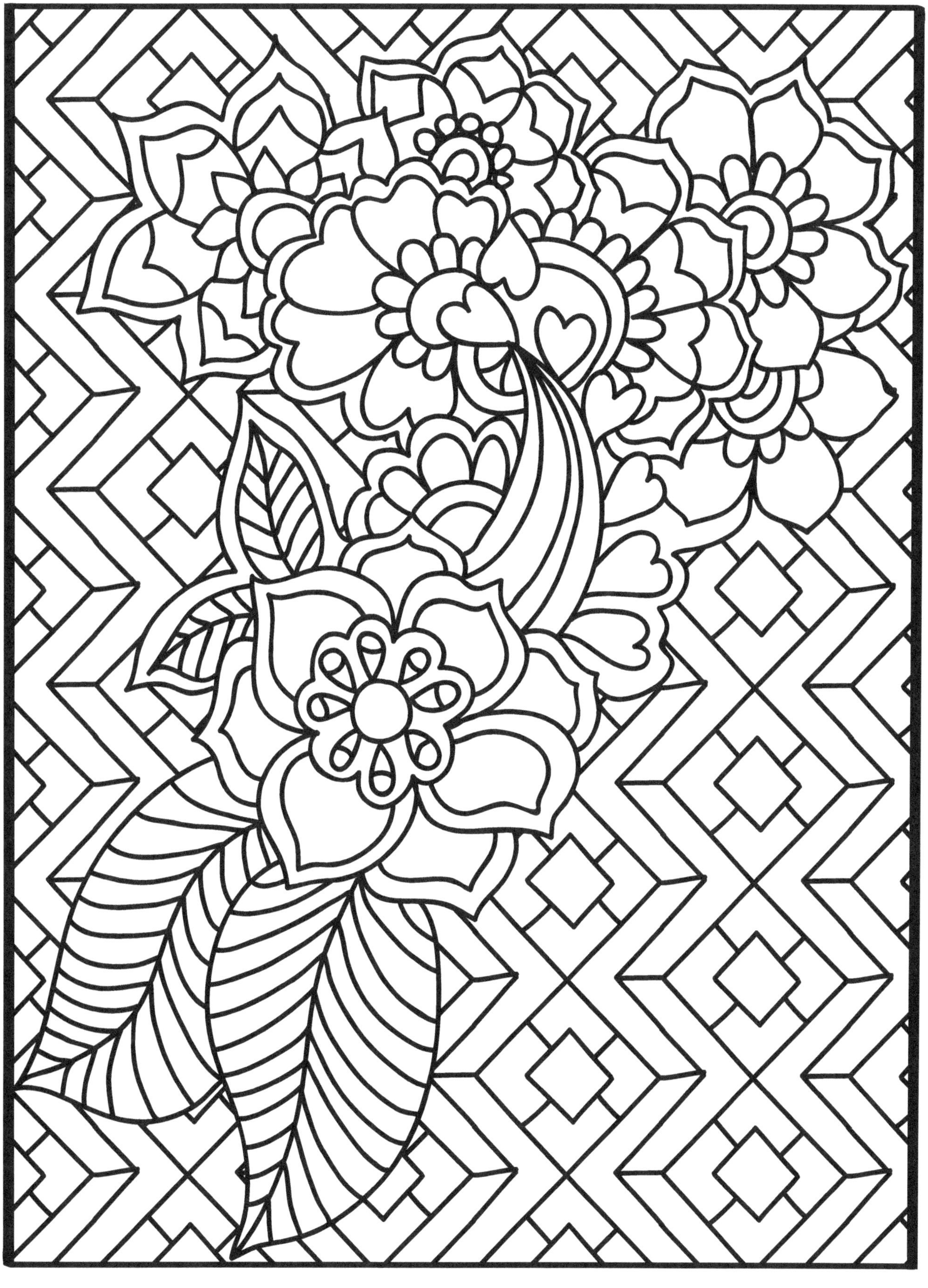

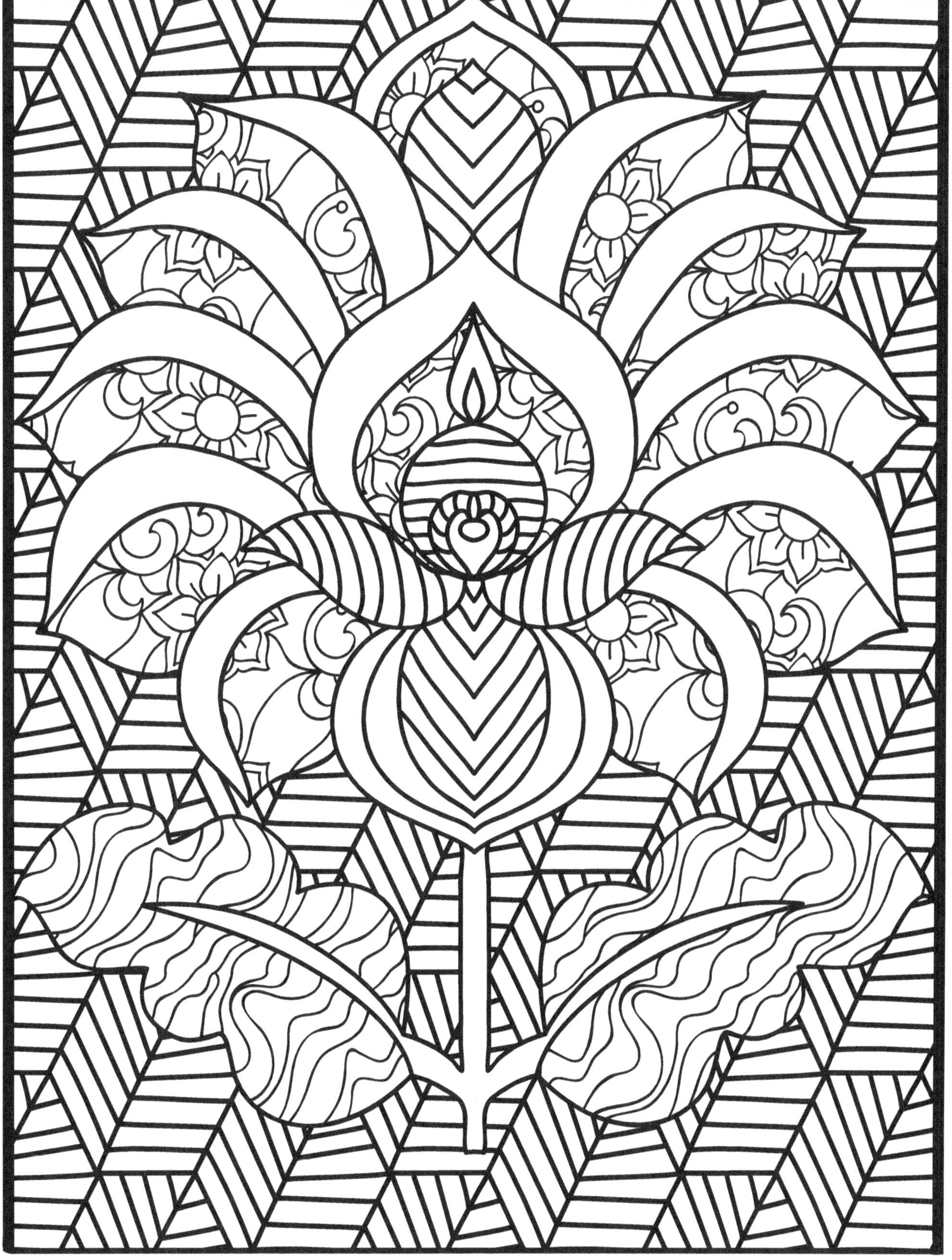

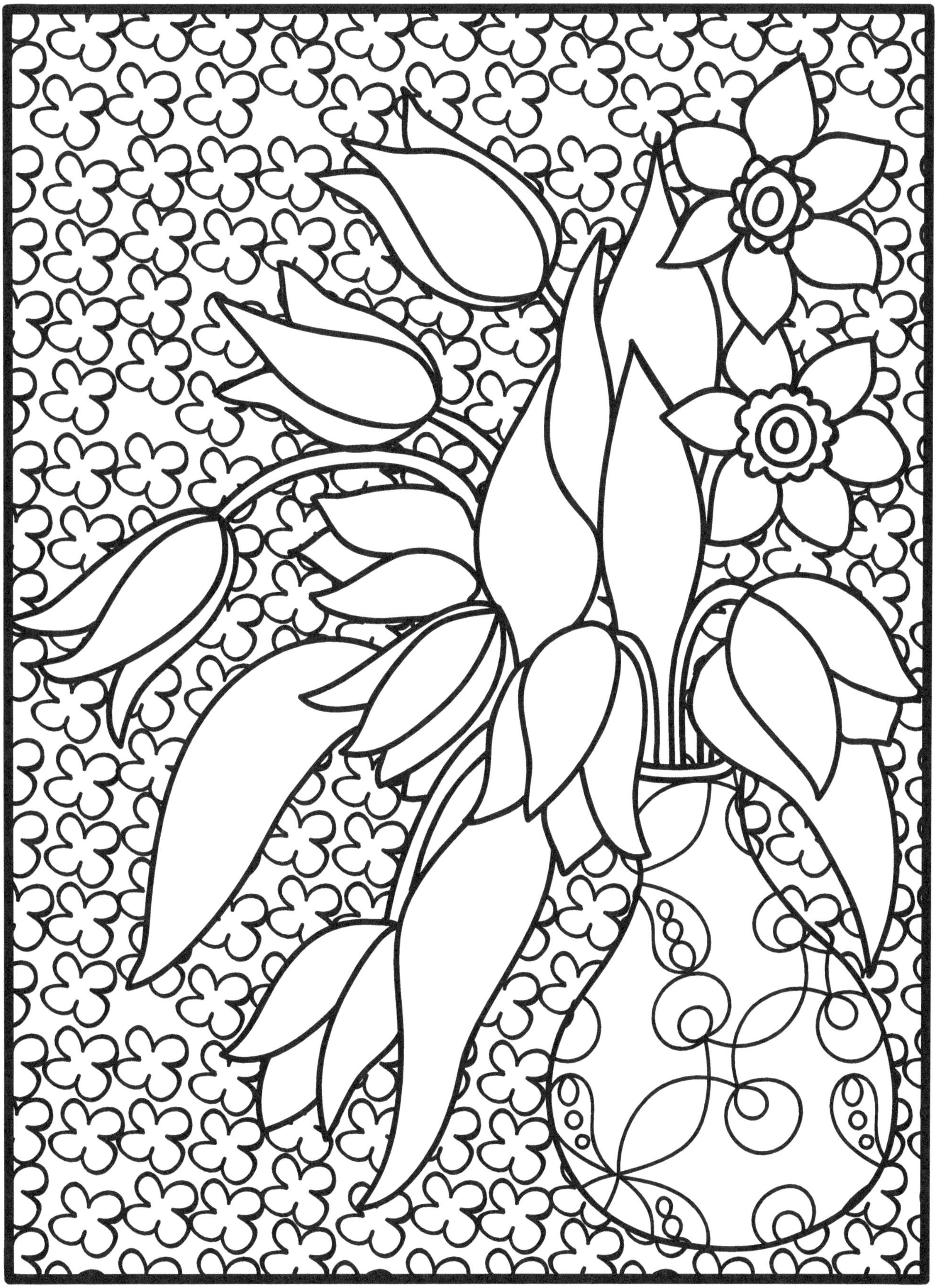

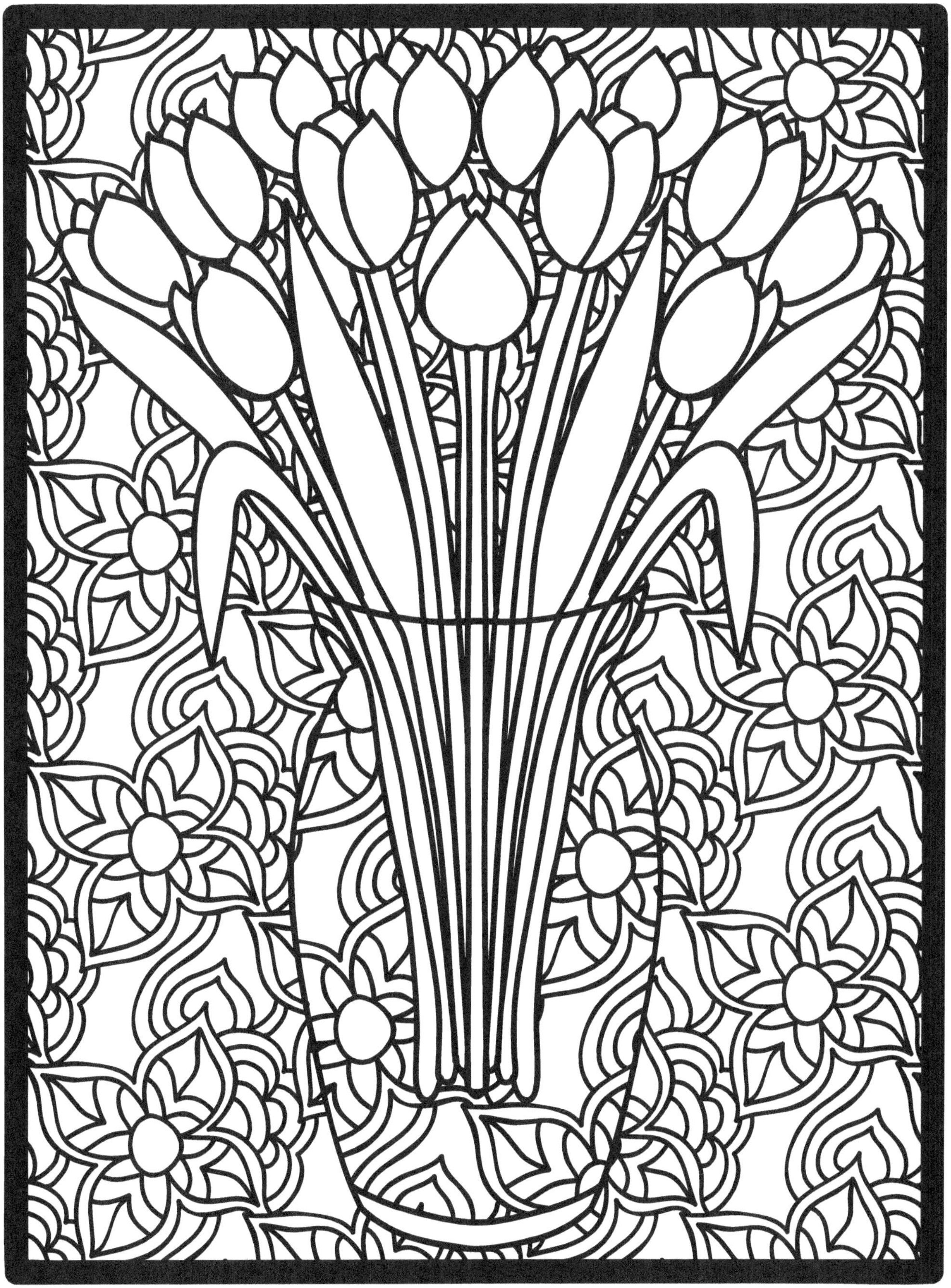

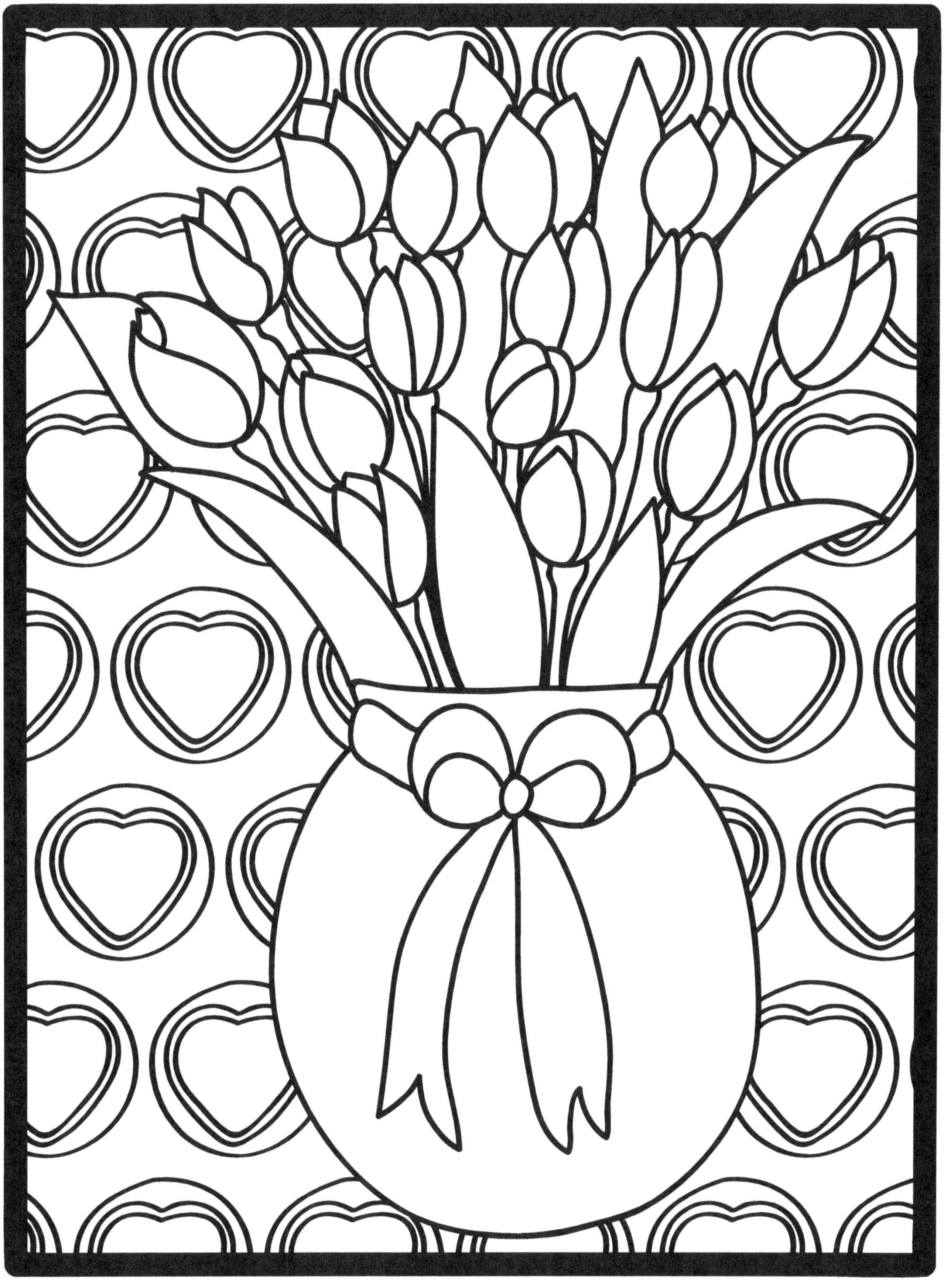

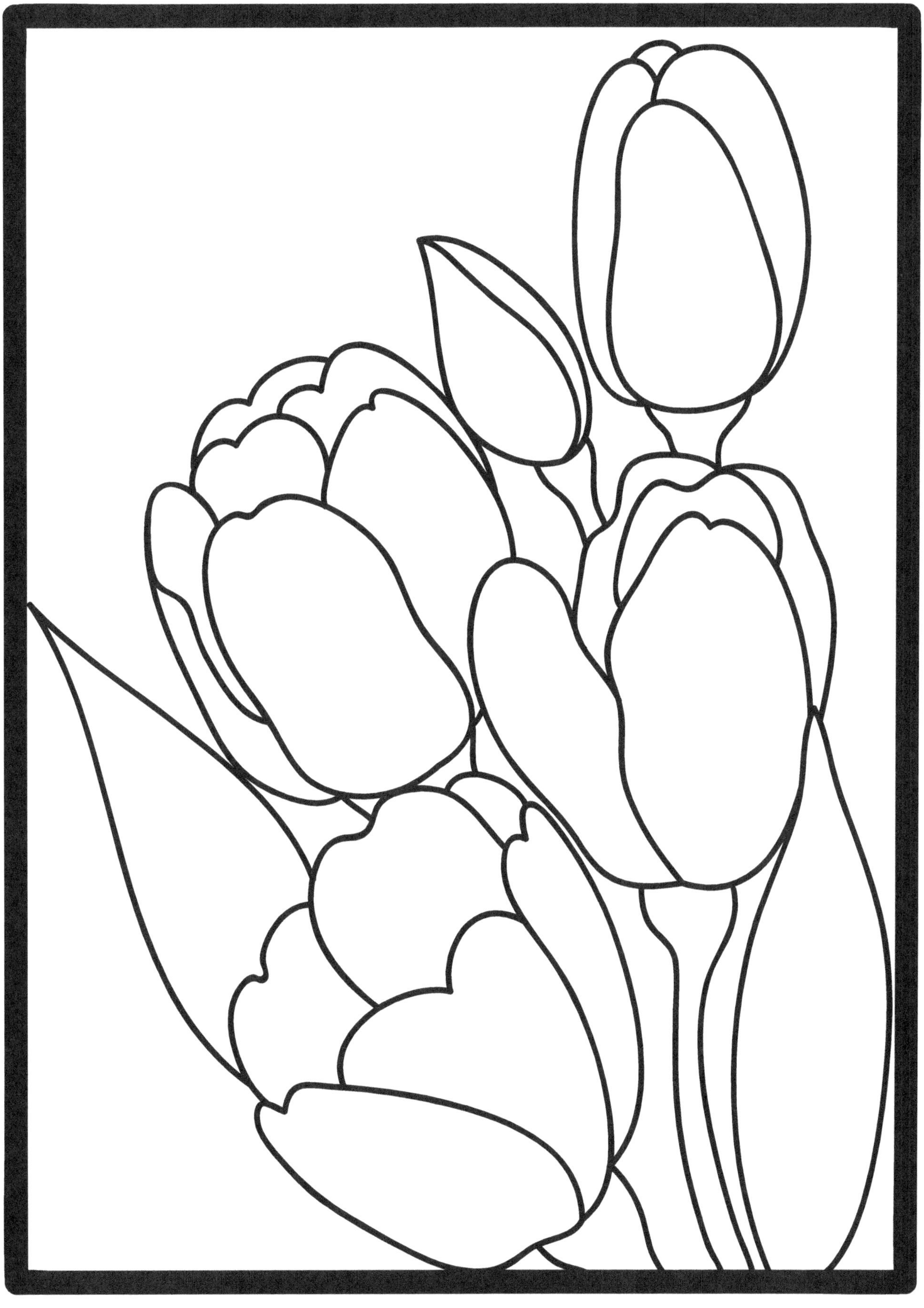

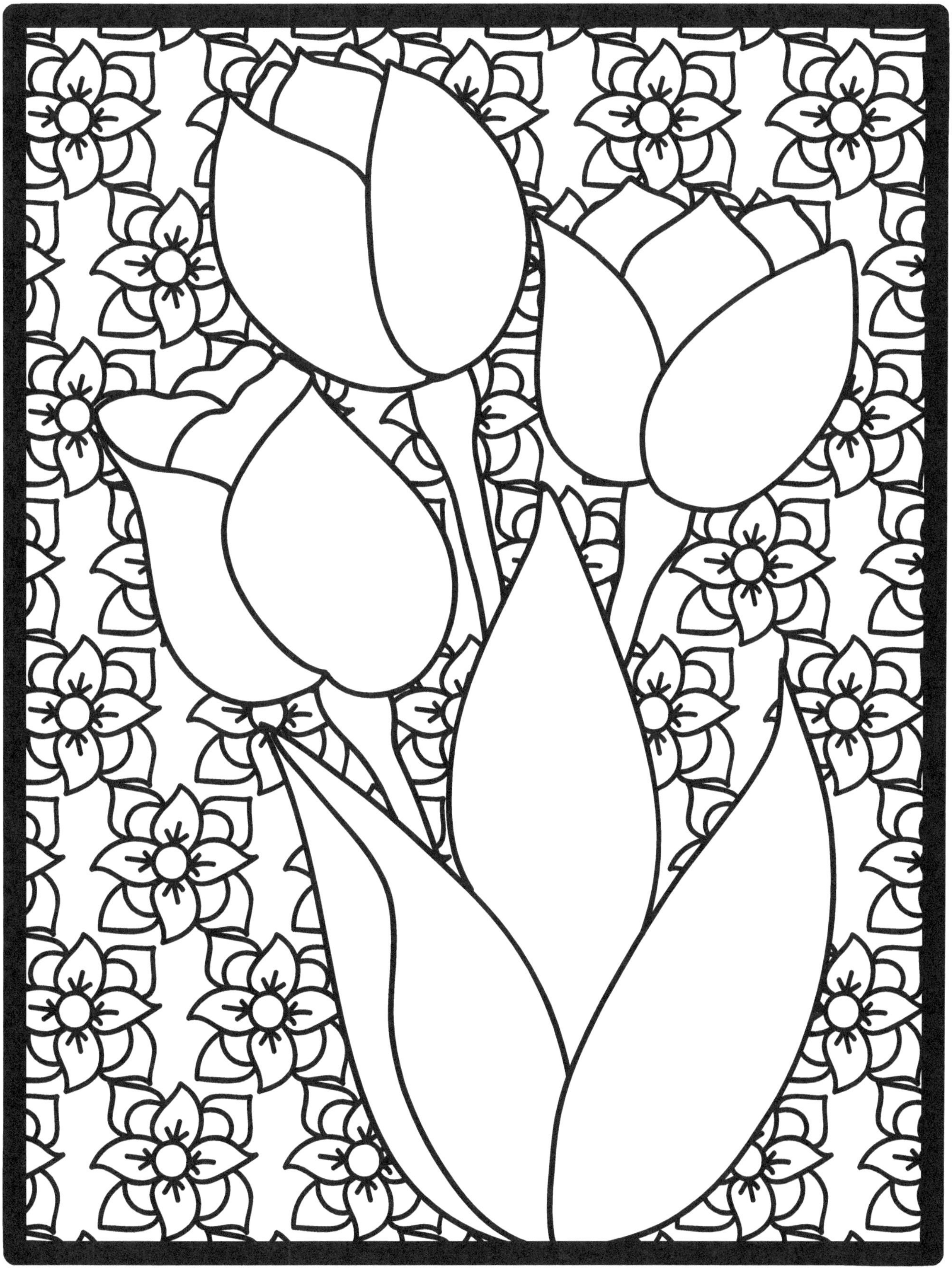

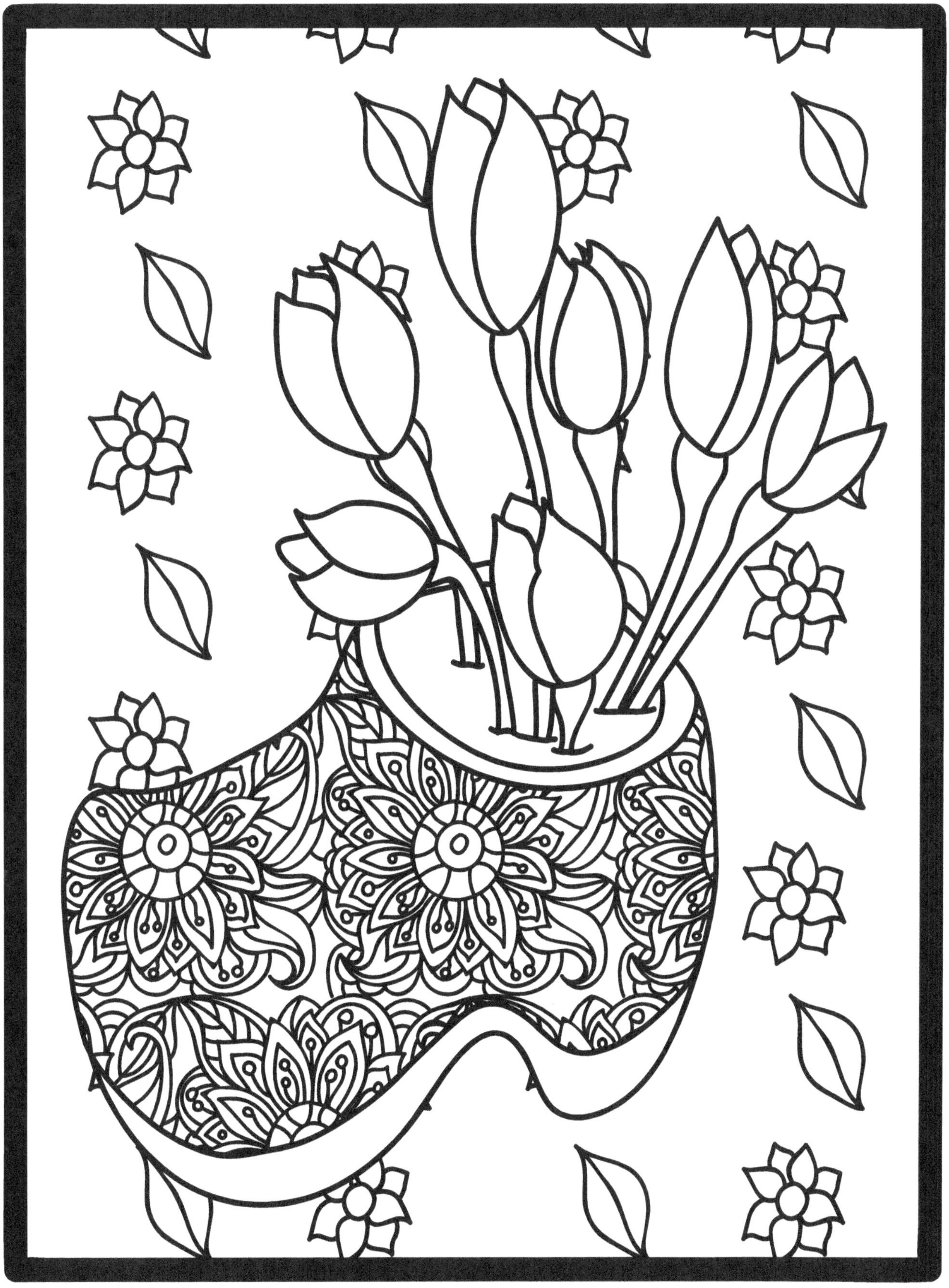

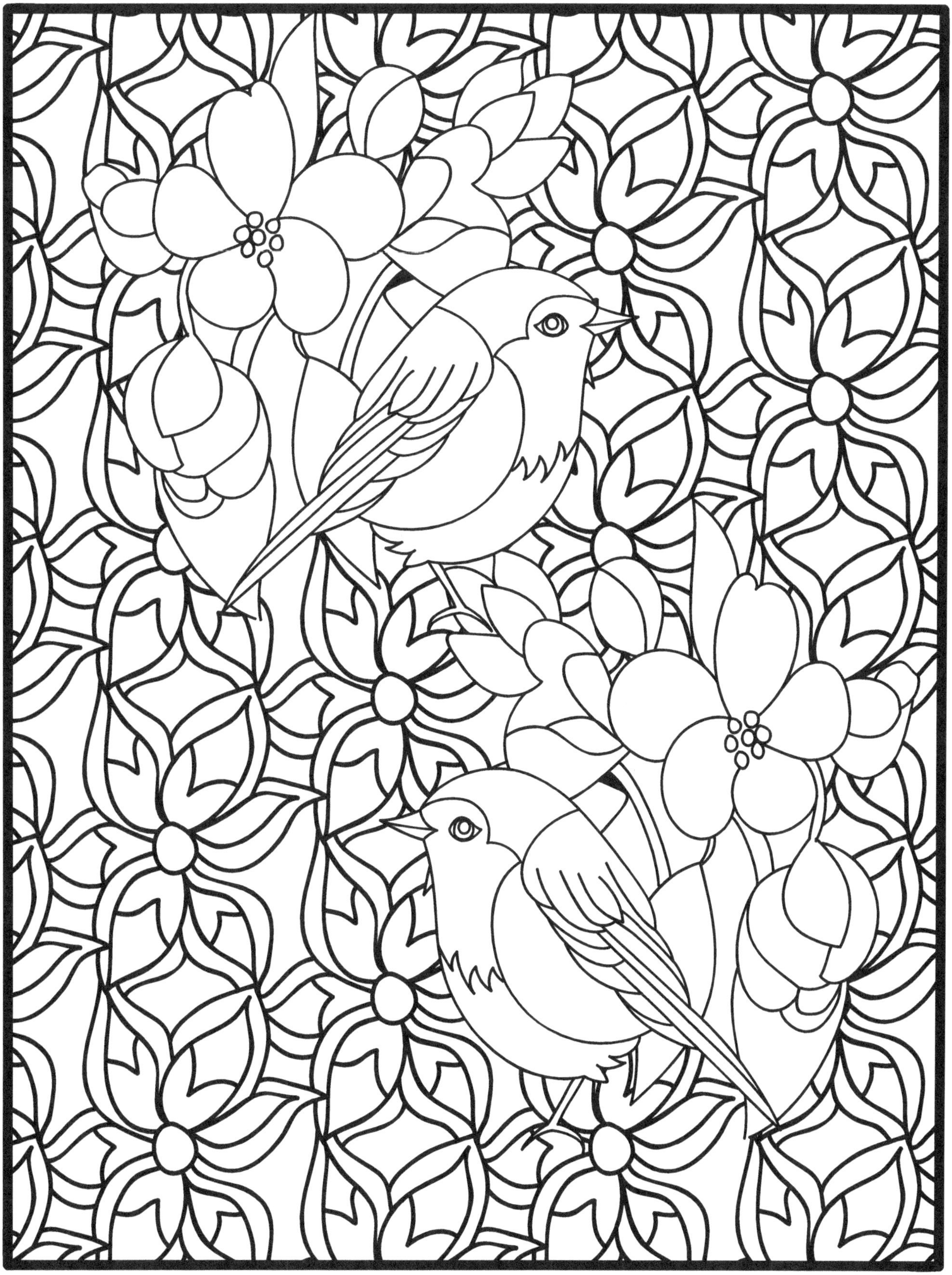

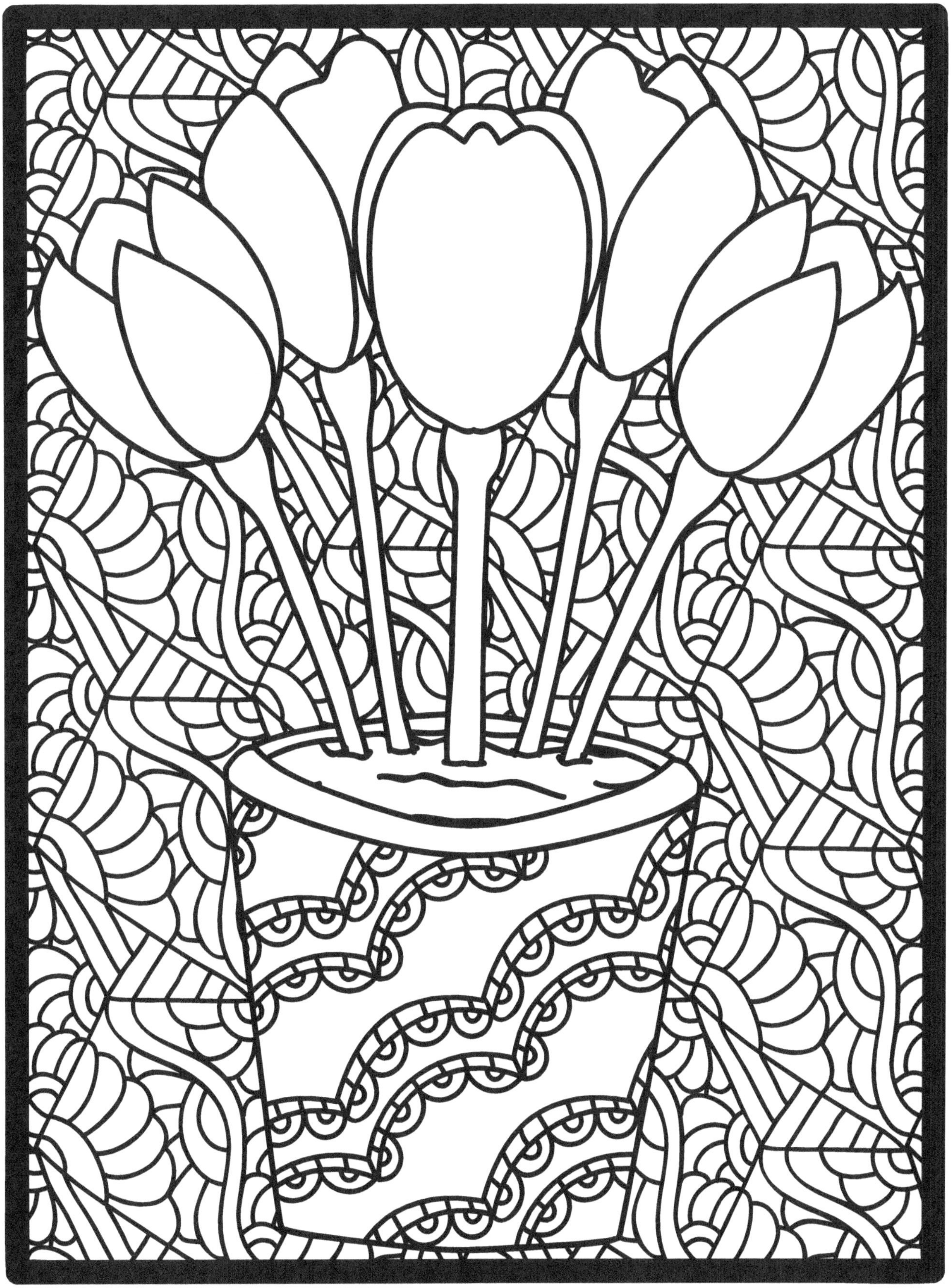

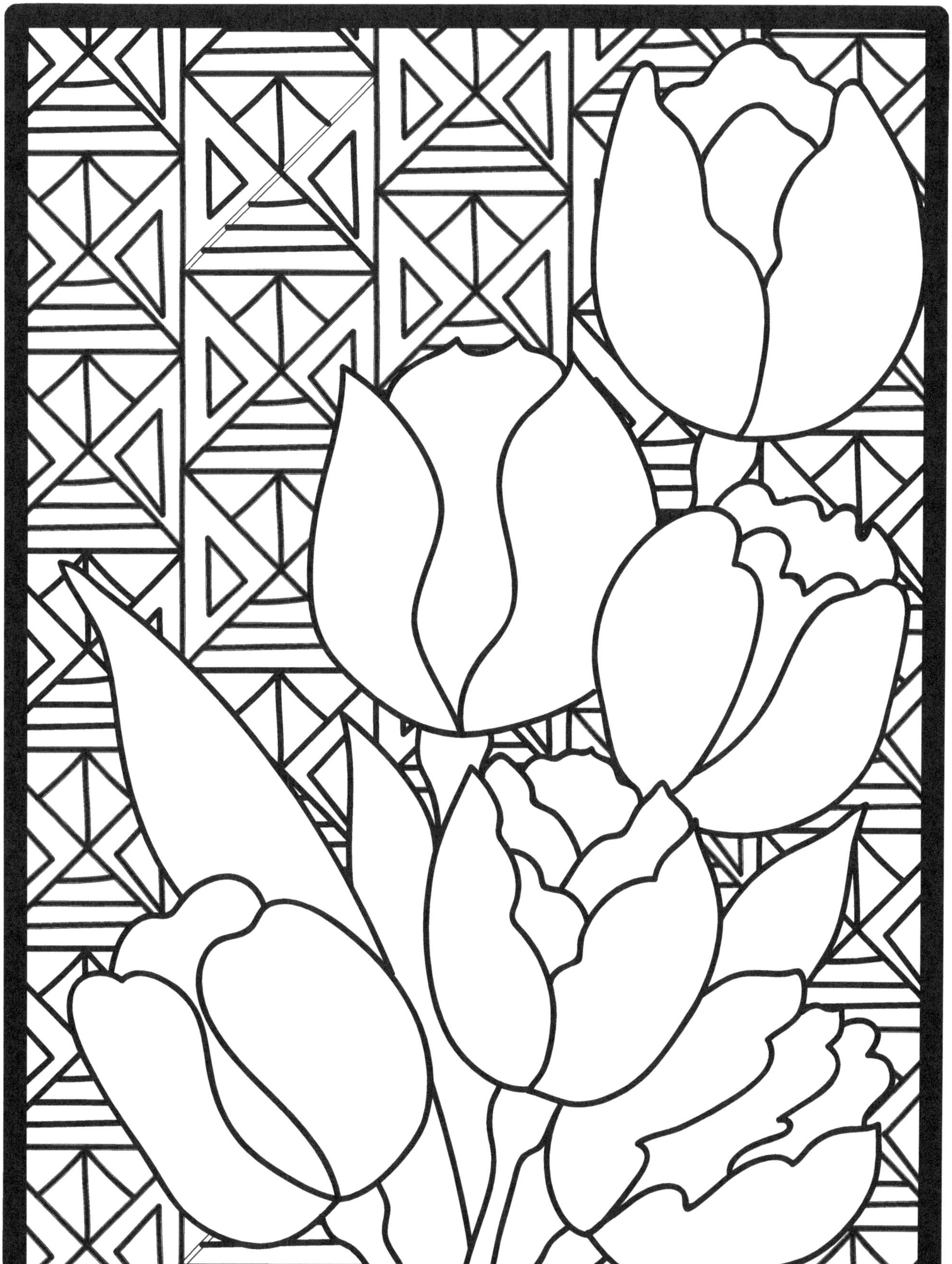

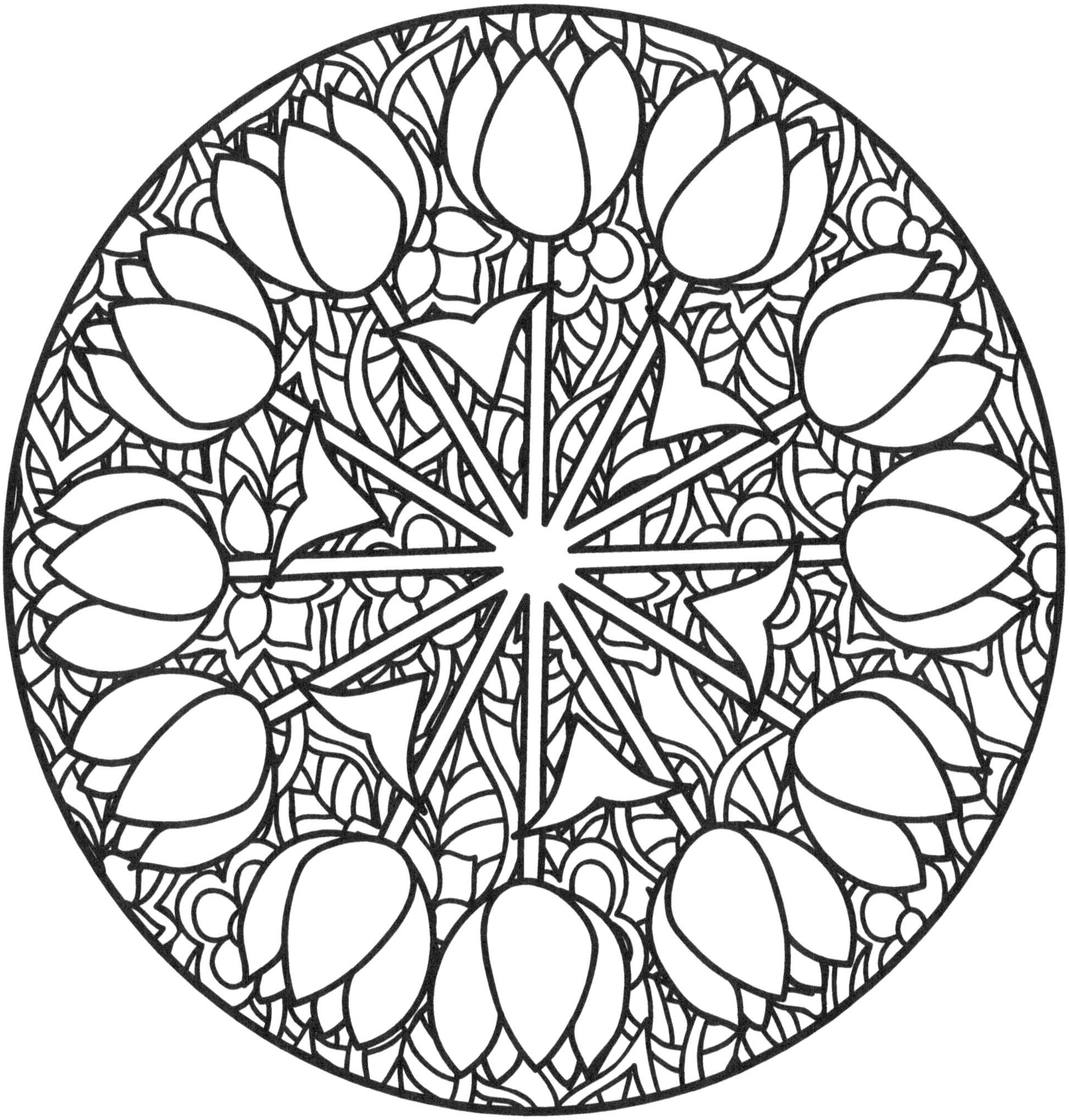

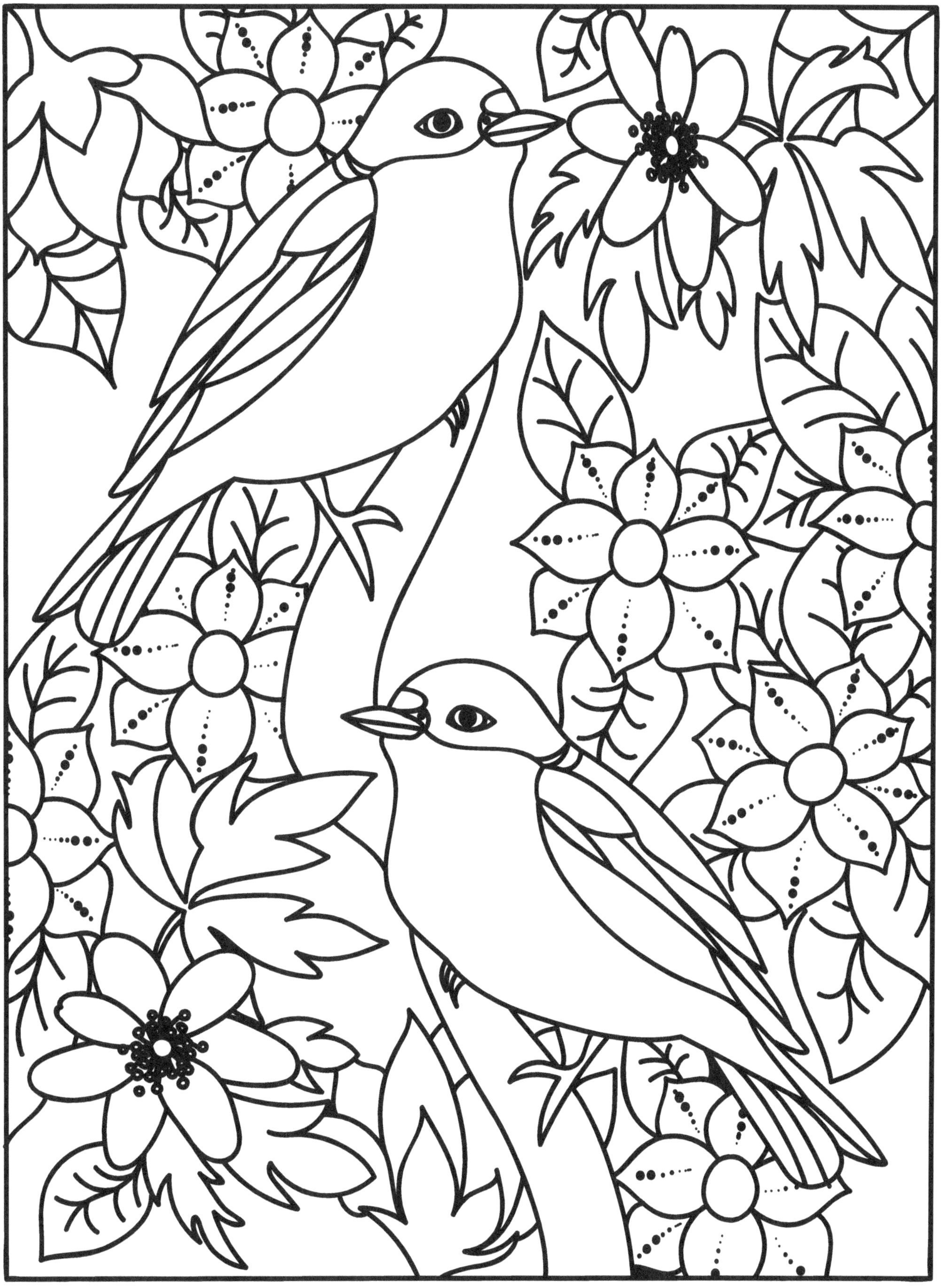

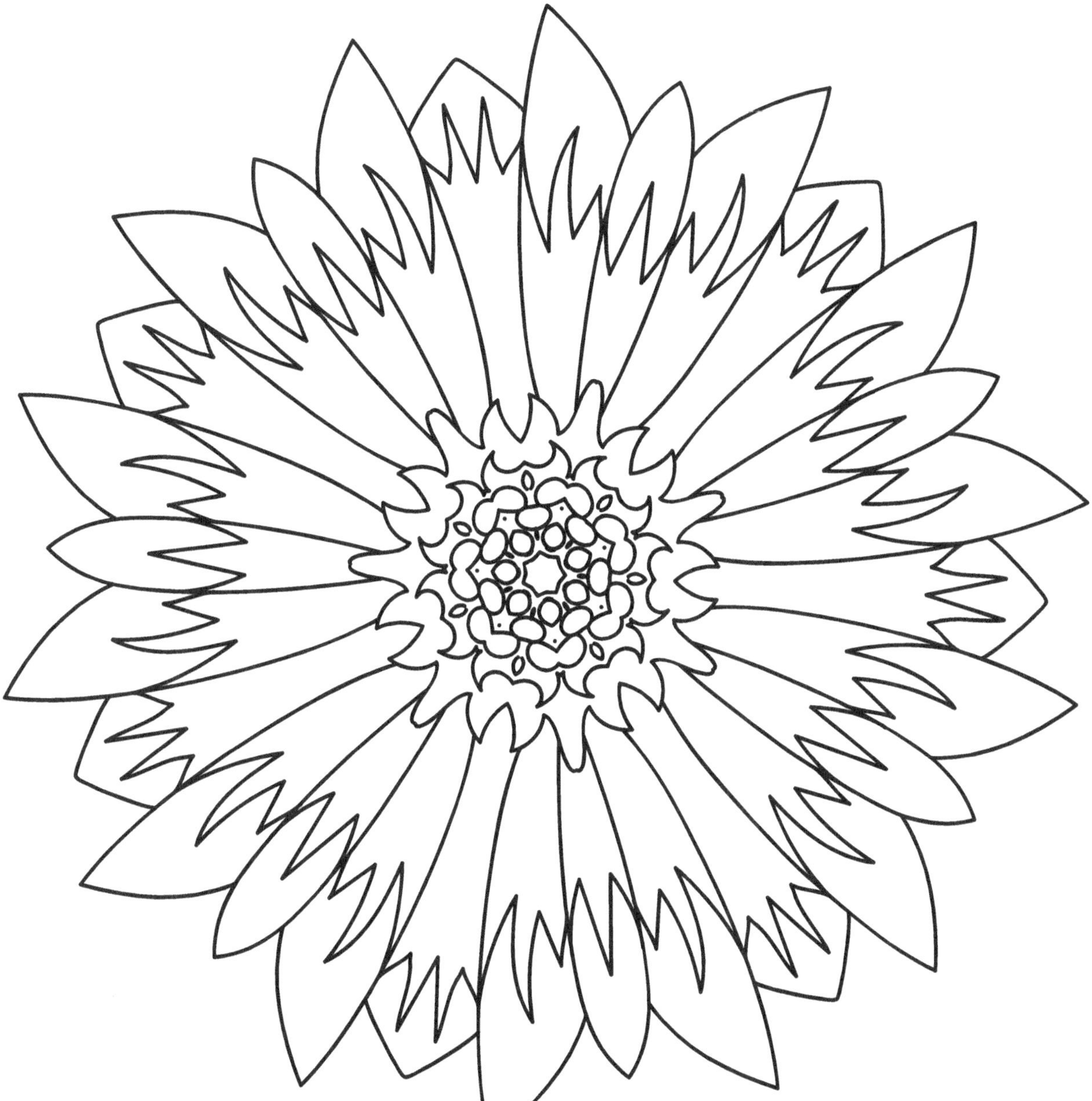

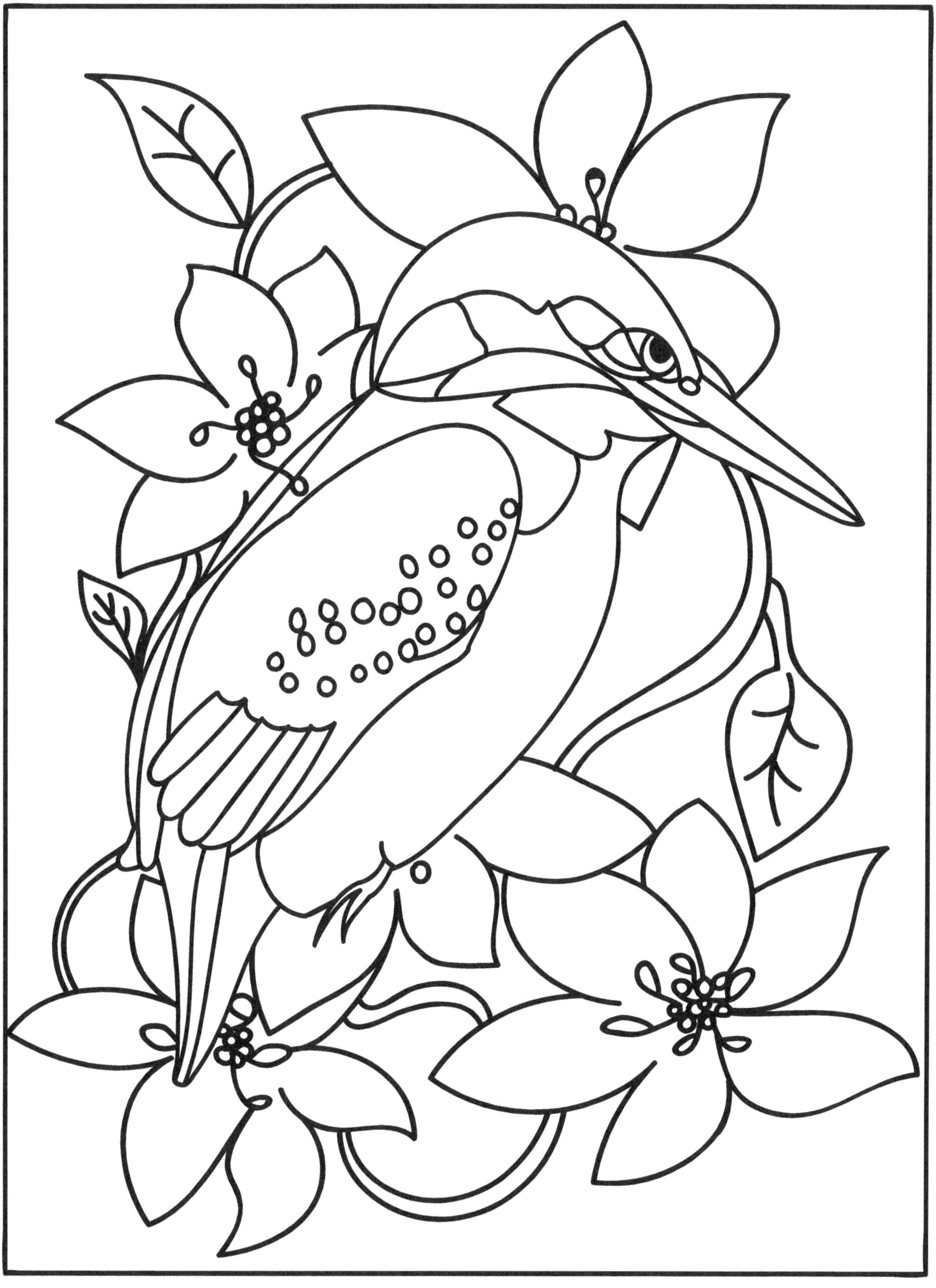

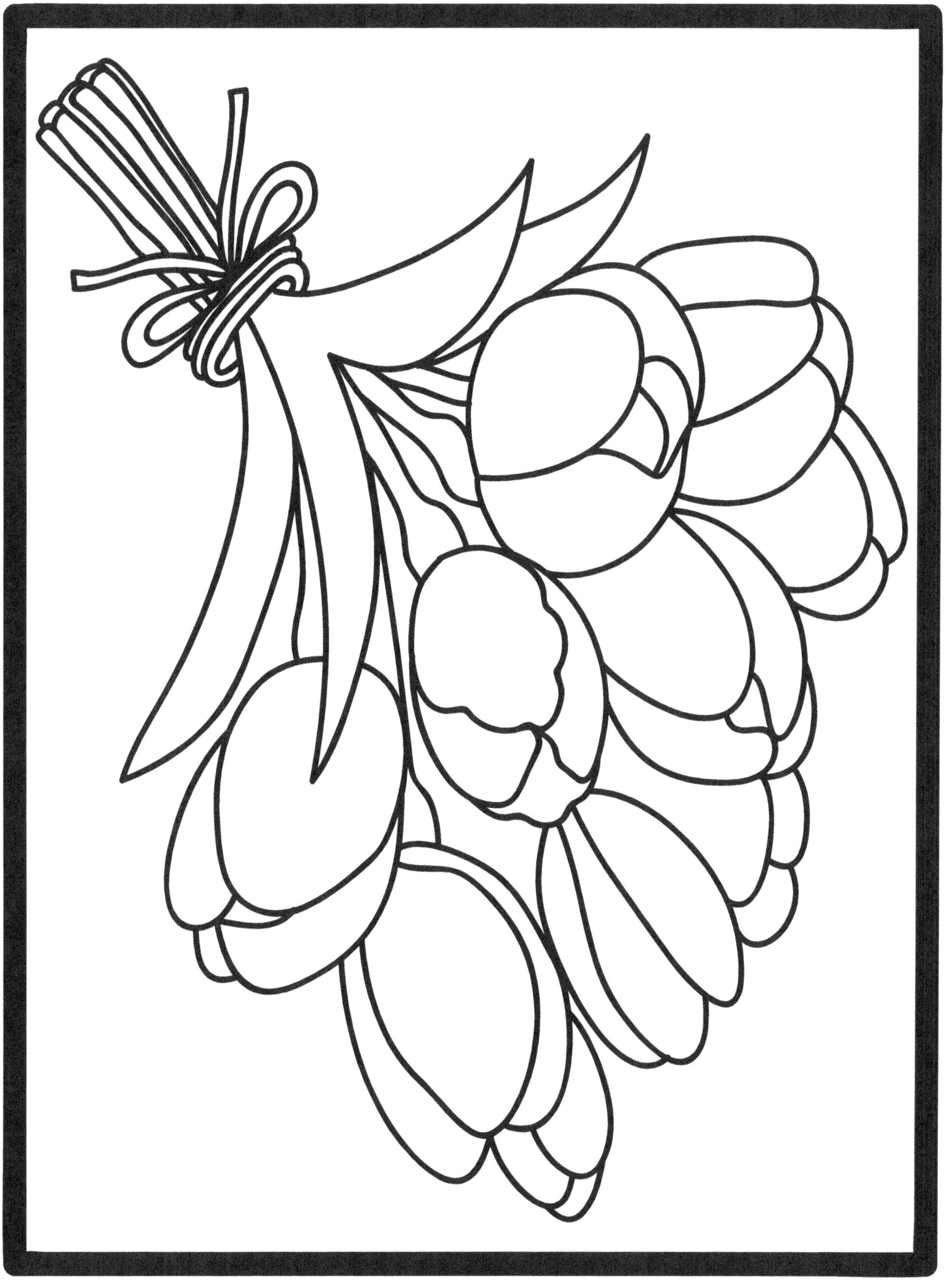

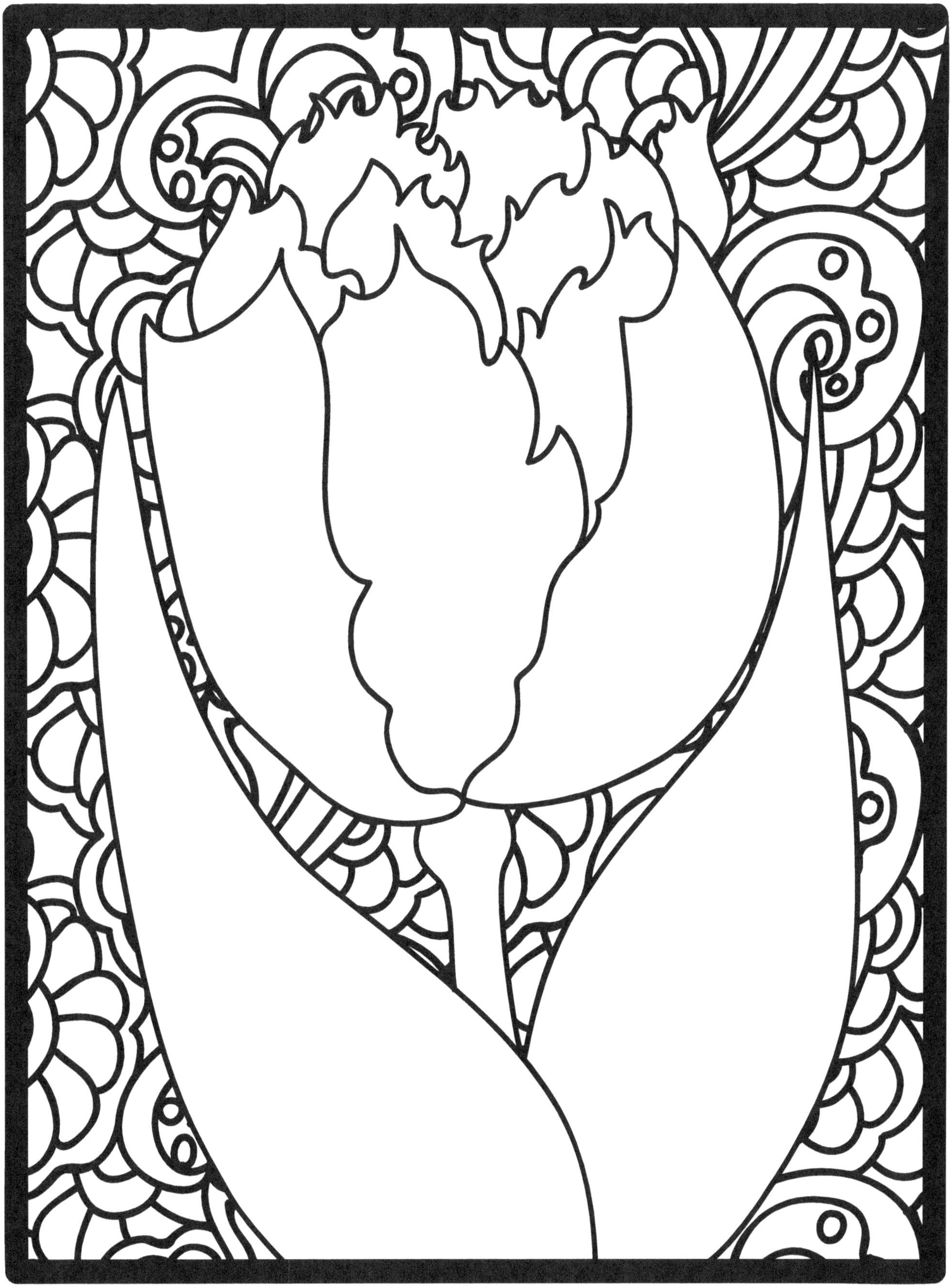

COLOR TEST PAGE

COLOR TEST PAGE

www.ingramcontent.com/pod-product-compliance
Lightning Source LLC
Chambersburg PA
CBHW082151230526
45467CB00044B/2838
9798692605900